"A rollicking good time, blendin[g] ... nod to the gods, and occasional ... confess, nowhere as comic as my own."

—Aristophanes, author of *Clouds* and *Frogs*

"If it is your fate to read this divine scroll, then whatever you do, don't run off to another city! That advised, you may not wish to read it in the company of your mother or father."

—Sophocles, inspired dramatist of the *Oedipus* cycle

"I'm thankful to the gods that Tim J. Young has written this slender volume before I perish and descend unto the dead. It's chock-full of solid *historia* (researches), so much so that I wish I had included more on wine in my own inquiries. Bravo, Young!"

—Herodotus of Halicarnassus, researcher of the *Histories*

"Although I'm not a fan of the 'You' in *Drinking Wine with Homer & the Earliest Greeks*, I can still recommend this fast reading scroll as the best compendium of its kind on Homeric drinking. Enjoy it with a cup of resinated red. You'll feel empowered to take care of your enemies and come out on top—*every* time!"

—Cleon, warmonger, demagogue, and all-around blowhard

"Not only does *Drinking Wine with Homer* achieve its *telos*, its goal, but it succeeds in helping the reader to achieve that *telos* for which all humans live … namely, happiness."

—Aristotle, author of the *Nicomachean Ethics*, *Politics*, and *Poetics*

"It's the kind of scroll I would have cherished before I died of the plague a few years ago. Now I'm sitting here forever in the dark, thirsting for just one drop of wine, and all I have is muddy water and the blues!"

—Pericles, Athenian statesman, orator, and general

"After questioning hundreds of ignorant men—poets, generals, businessmen, and duplicitous politicians—I've finally discovered one fellow who knows what he's talking about. Perhaps Apollo at the oracle at Delphi was mistaken after all. Or my dear friend Chaerephon. I can't say. Either way, I heartily recommend this scroll to you and to all your wine-loving (*philoinos*) friends. Cheers! I'll see you at the wine bowl!"

—Socrates, lover of wisdom, *philosophos*

"Don't tell anyone, but I secretly wish that I had written *Drinking Wine* for all the success it has given Tim J. Young. Doubtlessly he can now behave as a tyrant—though being the fool he is, he'll not take advantage of the power and will to pleasure at hand!"

—Thrasymachus, sophist, tyrant-want-to-be, and fan of Cleon

"If good cheer is balance, one indivisible atom together with another, then *Drinking Wine* will produce such an effect in your body and physical soul. We should know. We've both read it and have imbibed wine while delighting in its contents. Do likewise!"

—Democritus and Leucippus, chief creators of the atomist theory

Also by Tim J. Young

The One, the Many
A Novel of Constantine the Great, Athanasius of Alexandria, and
the Battle to Unify the Roman Empire
and the Christian Church

A Hero's Wish
What Homer Believed about
Happiness and the Good Life
(available mid-January 2015)

Drinking Wine with Homer & the Earliest Greeks

Drinking Wine with Homer & the Earliest Greeks

Cultivating, Serving & Delighting in Ancient Greek Wine

Including deliciously fun activities, Greek happiness formulas, and saucy suggestions for an ancient feast

Tim J. Young

Oinochoos Books
Sugar Land

DRINKING WINE WITH HOMER & THE EARLIEST GREEKS

Oinochoos Books, Sugar Land, TX 77479
www.oinochoosbooks.com

With SunWard Books
www.sunwardbooks.com

Cover design and all illustrations are by the author, but for the few that hail from the public domain.

ISBN 978-0-99-150611-8

This book was published in the United States of America.

Oinochoos Books is associated with SunWard Books and is a division of EuZōn Media
www.euzonmedia.com

FOR ALL MY COLLEGE FRIENDS
with whom I enjoyed many a jug of bad, bad wine—
I hope you have since learned to enjoy
the gift of Dionysus in a far more
fitting manner!

CONTENTS

INTRODUCTION

There is nothing better or more delightful than when a whole people make merry together ... while the table is loaded with bread and meats, and the cupbearer draws wine and fills it for every man.

—ODYSSEUS, THE *ODYSSEY*

HUMANS HAVE BEEN making and enjoying wines for millennia. Of them, the ancient Greeks seem to have especially delighted in wine. Homer stands out among the Greeks. Before the lyric poet Anacreon came along pouring out his life as a drink offering to the Muses, Eros, and the wine god Bacchus, declaring quite soberly that, "I have become a drinker," the epic poet Homer was stoking ancient Hellas' thirst with countless hexameter lines calling to mind Zeus' thundering rain, Gaia's fertile soil, Demeter's lush green vineyards pregnant with juicy grape clusters, and Dionysus' divine sparkling wine served in Hebe's golden goblets.

Have you ever wondered why reading the *Iliad* and the *Odyssey* make you want to get up, go to the wine rack, pop a cork, and decanter a bottle of red? (What, you haven't read these sacred poems recently? In case you didn't know, let me tell you that Homer was the go-to poet for how to live the good life for well over a thousand years. His epics were like the *Bible* for Christians, the *Mahabharata* for Hindus, and the *Heart Sutra* for Buddhists. Oh well. I suppose Homer has fallen on hard times.) Nevertheless, I challenge you to try it. Attempt reading Homer without getting that thirsty-for-wine craving. It's impossible.

The fact is the earliest Greeks, including our own dear poet, adored wine. Homer mentions it and wine related things hundreds of times throughout both epic poems. So do other early Greek poets, tragic and comic playwrights, historians, doctors, sophists, politicians, and early philosophers. Not to mention the average Joe (aka *Iosēph*). In Plato's *Republic*, Socrates asserts that most people equate the good life with one where they can frequently wine, dine, and concubine. As one historian remarked, ancient Greece was a wine culture, driven by its love for the fruit of Dionysus. So let's be inspired by this love and adoration!

The proposal of this small, lighthearted book is very simple. The more you know about wine, the more you'll enjoy drinking it. The project's adventure, then, is to join Homer and the earliest Greeks in their experience and enjoyment of wine.

In order to do so, we'll explore a number of questions. What did the earliest Greeks believe about wine's origins? How did they cultivate the vine and make wine? How did wine circulate throughout Greece and the broader Mediterranean world? What did wine do for Homer's heroes and other early Greeks? Lastly, how did drinking fit in with the variety of formulas for happiness in ancient Hellas?

But for now, forget about all these questions. While you read along, I want you to know that you're no longer you. Let that sink in for a moment while you take a swallow of your favorite grape based beverage.

Who are you? Glad you asked.

You're an Athenian citizen living during the fifth year of the Peloponnesian War. It's 427 BC. You're married, have four children—three boys and a girl—and your relationship with your wife is as close as Hector's was with Andromache in Troy or Odysseus' was with Penelope in Ithaca (despite the general male orientation of the world you live in).

It's summer and hot. But thank the air-condition god Zephyrus, a wind is blowing from the west.

You're strolling along with Herodotus through the vineyard on your farm just outside Athens. Although the soil is rocky, thin, and poor for wheat and barley, the vines thrive as they always do under your direction and your servant's care. You're proud as you lift a new cluster of green grapes to show the old man. *Zeus!* Give them another few months and they'll be fat and dark purple, ready to harvest and make wine.

From his response, Herodotus seems impressed. Again, you're proud. Given his intelligence and widespread knowledge, this is no small thing.

The old man is giving a reading of his inquiries later on tonight at your friend Hipponicus' house in Athens. You plan to be there. Although you've already heard much of what Herodotus is likely to share since he's been your guest before, you're excited to hear a more formal presentation of his account of the epic war between the Greeks and the barbarian Persians. And let's admit it, you could use a night out drinking with your friends.

As you pass through the vineyard's wooden gate set in the gray stone wall you rebuilt last year, dusty stone weighed down by dusty stone, and over the earthen dyke piled high on the other side, and up the dirt path to your house, Herodotus asks you how your farm escaped the Peloponnesian offensive over the summer. Their vandalism. You tell him that you credit the gods and the fact that the Spartans were intent upon moving on quickly to Lesbos to help the rebellious Mytilenians.

He sighs. "I understand there will be a vote in a few days in your assembly whether to punish the Mytilenians or not for what they've done."

Now you sigh. "It's true. And gods, I'd rather not think about it. When will this bitter war ever end?"

(Sorry, but as someone from the future, I can confidently tell you that you have another twenty-three years to go.)

You reach your house and sit beneath the shade of a gnarled tree that's been on the farm for generations. Herodotus reclines next to you, stretching out his legs and wrinkled feet from beneath his light tunic. His toes look like grapes left out to dry in the sun.

Wine?

He nods.

Soon enough a servant brings you a resinated red to sip along with goat cheese, olives, figs, onions, bread, and olive oil to snack on. After pouring out a libation and briefly hymning Hestia and Demeter, you drink.

Aside from making your way from your farm into town later on—past the Kerameikos, the agora, and on to Hipponicus' house by the Acropolis—this is what you hope to do the rest of the day and night until, as Homer so often says, you've thrown aside all desire for food and drink.

Something dark purple and fragrant tells you you're going to succeed. That, and Herodotus will make a good companion. If only you didn't have to think about the upcoming vote in the assembly and what it might mean for you. *Curses!*

Oh well. You can't help what will happen. As the Stoics will later say, it's out of your control. You can only enjoy yourself right now.

Deliciously Fun Activity No. 1

Reading Homer and testing the
Homer-Causes-a-Desire-for-Wine hypothesis

Step one. If you haven't read Homer's *Iliad* or *Odyssey* for a long time, pick up a copy of each from your local bookstore (do these exist anymore?), library, or your favorite online retailer (presently dominating the world market).

For a flowing, highly readable translation, I recommend Robert Fagles' version (Penguin Books). If you prefer one that's faithful to the Greek, however, go with Richmond Lattimore (U. Chicago Press for the *Iliad* and Harper Perennial for the *Odyssey*). Otherwise, if you're hankering for side-by-side Greek and English, then Harvard's portable and dear-to-my-soul mantis green Loeb Classics will do the trick (Homer in four volumes, translated by A.T. Murray and revised by George E. Dimock). If these don't work and you're hard up for cash, several online editions are available. The University of Chicago offers a Greek-English searchable version (R. Lattimore's *Iliad* and James Huddleston's *Odyssey*), and many websites make available the late Victorian Samuel Butler translation from some one hundred and more years ago. If you want a little more rhythm and rhyme in your read, you can find online Alexander Pope's eighteenth century translation in heroic couplets. Check out the first lines of the *Iliad*:

> *Achilles' wrath, to Greece the direful spring*
> *Of woes unnumber'd, heavenly goddess, sing!*
> *That wrath which hurl'd to Pluto's gloomy reign*
> *The souls of mighty chiefs untimely slain!*

Step two. Once you've scored your copy of Homer, then read. It's as simple as that. But don't hurry! Sit in your favorite armchair or outside if it's sunny or inside if you're

in North Dakota and enjoy every word. And when you're done, repeat. Homer is like that cult film you and your good friends enjoyed in high school or college. The more you read him, the better he gets. And, admittedly, the longer you read, the more you want to throw down a glass of wine—which brings me to the third and essential part of the deliciously fun activity.

Step three. Remember the very serious challenge I made a few pages back? Try it. Try reading Homer without feeling thirsty for wine.

My sincere promise: If you can successfully peruse the epics without this particular grape-inspired thirst, then email me and I'll respond congratulating you on not having any alcoholic tendencies.

Or aunts or uncles.

Then I'll feel sorry for you (but I won't write that).

AMPHORA I

CULTIVATING, PREPARING, AND SERVING
ANCIENT GREEK WINE

1

THE GIFT OF THE GODS

I was seized with desire ... and Semele bore Dionysus, the joy of mortals.
—ZEUS, THE *ILIAD*

U P AND DOWN YOU go. Back you pull. Relax. Sweat
drips from your dark curly hair and brows down your
tanned face into your wavy beard and onto your stripped
down, glistening body. It's hot beneath the summer sun.

It's four days later now, and you're aboard a trireme with
two hundred other men, most of them rowers like you.
Otherwise, the sailors guide the sails, the piper keeps the
time, the *kubernētēs* steers the ship,
and spearmen and archers wait idly
by while the trierarch gladly shouts
out that you're nearing Lesbos.

It's dawn. You're on a mission that you'd rather not be
on—but curse it all to Tartaros, you're a citizen of Athens,
and so you'll do what the assembly has ordered even if you
voted against it. (Is that even ethical?)

Two days ago, after a hasty gathering punctuated by impatient fury, your fellow Athenians ordered a trireme to
Mytilene, the chief *polis* on the island of Lesbos. The

mission? There, the trierarch would order the Athenian commander Paches to slay all the men for Spartan support-ed rebellion and enslave all the women and children for being married and born to the wrong men.

According to the rising star and ape-man Cleon, a politi-cal demagogue you despise, your city has to remind others that its empire is a despotism. His words, not yours. So there's no room for mercy. Even though you strongly disagree with him and prefer Diodotus' more tolerant position, you're nonetheless on your way. *Lucky you.*

As you row back and forth, you consider how gruesome the task will be, slaughtering so many men. A line from Homer zips into your head as if sent by a god. It likens the making of wine to the bloody press of war and fighting. Wine and blood. Popping grapes; punctured men. As a later historian of religion will write, "The association of red wine with blood is widespread and very ancient."

Gods, you want some wine. You desperately need some-thing reinvigorating, something to take your mind off the nasty business at hand. You'll be there all too soon.

Given your destination, you remember one of Mytilene's most famous poets. No, not the woman Sappho—the lesbian Lesbian. Even though as a poet she claimed an equal status to Homer, she's not the one.

As you pull and relax, pull and relax, you think about him, the poet Alcaeus of Mytilene, who composed many entertaining drinking songs. He begins one by shouting, "Let's drink!"

If only.

He goes on to declare that wine is the gift of the gods, and of one blessed god in particular. "For the son of Semele and Zeus granted men wine to forget their cares."

That's exactly what you need. A little care-relieving wine. A little Dionysus to cheer up your mood. A little fire to burn off the early morning patches of fog you and the other men are cutting through to make it to the island that must be just over the horizon.

Suddenly it comes! As if in response to your desire, Helios rides higher into the sky, and his fiery rays set aglow the surrounding fog, slowly burning it off.

Now you pass through golden clouds of water vapor and sunshine, much like the cloud Zeus created to hide his love making with his wife-sister Hera hundreds and hundreds of years ago during the tenth year of the Trojan War. As you recall it from Homer's telling in the *Iliad*, it was quite a roll.

"Hera baby," Zeus calls out from the heights of Mount Ida, "I want you like I've never wanted a mortal woman or an immortal goddess before!"

Hera rolls her gold-painted eyes.

"Well, maybe there were a few others…"

She rolls them the other way.

Zeus goes on to boast about all the ladies he'd bedded. It's a regular testosterone-fuelled locker-room glory report. Let's see: there was Danae, Europa, Alcmene, Demeter, Leto, and Ixion's wife—what was her name?—and Semele, he brags toward the end, divine pecks flexed, who gave birth to Dionysus, the delight (*charma*) of mortals.

Your dry throat contracts as you longingly swallow. *Wine!*

Dionysus, God of Wine

Although Homer says little more about Dionysus, other early Greek literature fills in the gap. One of the Homeric hymns reveals, for instance, that when the god disclosed himself to a group of sailors, he was youthful in appearance and beautiful. His hair was dark, perhaps the color of the dark skin of a grape. Around his strong shoulders, he wore a purplish-red cloak. The Greek word is *porphureos*, which comes from the purple-fish, *Murex trunculus* (*porphura*), from which dyers made Tyrian or Royal purple in antiquity. Another hymn adds that he was "ivy-crowned."

We can imagine the god, then, with ivy twisted upon his dark head, like grapevines flourishing around purple clusters of round fruit. He is "Dionysus, rich in grapes." And if you dare to venture into a wooded valley, you may find him dancing about with his diaphanously clad maenads, the god "wreathed with ivy and bay leaves" and carrying the *thyrsos*, a pinecone topped fennel staff wrapped with ivy.

Dionysus' Parents and Birth

Whatever he looked like and whatever joy he brought, Hera didn't care too much for the lad or for any other of Zeus' children that were not her own.

Why should she? Moreover, she didn't like that little dog-eyed mother of the god. The slut! But it wasn't Semele's fault!

It's not like she had much to say about the matter. According to Hesiod's *Theogony*, she "yielded to Zeus' lust." Was she forced? Hard to say. Either way, her luck (or bad luck) didn't end when Zeus' lustful eyes zeroed in on her like lightning. No, somehow, when she slept with Zeus, his hot thunderbolt burned her up! One minute she was there making love to the father of gods and men; the next, poof, she was gone!

Before she vanished, though, Zeus managed to save the fruit of her womb. Through the smoke, he snatched Dionysus from Semele's sizzling, double-t hott body that she'd spent hours working out for, and then he did the obvious thing: he sewed the young divinity into his thigh.

Sometime later, Zeus gave birth to the god in a mysterious spot. As one of the Homeric hymns reports the joyous event, the newly born lad cried out, "I am loud-shouting [*eribromos*] Dionysus"—from which we get his nickname, Bromius (aka the original Bro)—"born to Semele, the daughter of Cadmus, who mingled in love with Zeus."

With Dionysus' booming revelation, we learn about his mother's side of the family. As he gives it, Semele was the daughter of Cadmus, who was the king of Thebes in Boeotia (in central Greece) and the grandson of Poseidon, who rules the sea and shakes the earth. Thebes was later famous for Oedipus, who, thanks to Fate, murdered his father and married his own mother before eventually blinding himself and becoming a sage like the seer rock star Tiresias. He was Semele's great-grandnephew.

As for Dionysus' father's side, Zeus' was the third major generation of gods "from the beginning" after the two headed by Ouranos-Gaia and Kronos-Rheia. His grandmother was the great Earth-Mother Gaia who was there along with Chaos and Desire-Eros at the very beginning. Unfortunately, both his grandfather and father wished to halt the evolution of the cosmos, thereby asking for serious trouble (you can't do that).

Ouranos did so by stuffing his offspring back into Gaia. He paid a stiff price for this, however, with the loss of his *ahem* member. When IT fell to the sea, the Erinyes, Giants, and Nymphs were born from the wound's dripping blood, and Aphrodite was generated from the splashing foam rising up from the sinking genitals (*mēdos*, a word referring

to both the genitals and a man's plans. *Interesting*). Kronos, the one who lopped off his father's penis, apparently didn't learn much from the incident. Rather, he grumpily went on to swallow his own children, enacting his own version of cosmos-pause (take that, Neil deGrasse Tyson!).

Well, just as Fate didn't favor his own father, neither did it favor Kronos. After a ferociously violent battle, Zeus seized control of Mount Olympus from the previous generation of gods, the Titans, including his own father Kronos. In the end, after he imprisoned them in Tartaros, he had his way with everything, including Hera (most of the time) and mortal beauties like Semele.

But where was Dionysus born? And once born, how did he make his way to ancient Hellas? To ask these questions is to ask where and when humans first fermented wine, or at least when they discovered the fact that grape juice could magically morph into an enticingly intoxicating liquid, and how this liquid migrated to Greece. To answer the question, we have to explore two sources. One is myth, the stories and legends purportedly relating the truth about the god's origins and appearance. The other is the witness of history, and most notably, the archeological record.

Dionysus' Birth Place and Path to Greece

Ancient Greek mythology grants us many different answers to the 'where the god was born' question, but two stand out as common. In Euripides' tragedy *The Bacchae*, Dionysus claims that he was born in Thebes. Not true, counters the first *Homeric Hymn to Dionysus*. Rather, the god of the vine was born far away from Thebes in Nysa, "in a distant part of Phoenicia, almost at the waters of the river Nile."

But where in Gaia's green earth is this? Given the broad and ambiguous coordinates, Nysa could be located anywhere from modern Syria down to the Sinai Peninsula of Egypt. So, where?

Intriguingly, according to a study prepared by the archaeologist Virginia R. Grace for the American School of Classical Studies, ceramic vessels that held and transported wine likely came from roughly the same geographical area. "The idea of a two-handled pottery container made especially for transport seems to have originated with the Canaanites"—yes, those of Biblical fame, the ones cursed by Noah because his son Ham, the father of Canaan, guiltily espied the antediluvian patriarch naked when Noah was drunk on wine he'd made from his own vineyard. (Thank the gods, despite the dubious logic, we now understand why the Canaanites were the ones perpetually harassed by the Israelites.) In any event, V.R. Grace goes on to explain that the Canaanites were the "forefathers of the Phoenicians, in the coastal area of later Syria and Palestine." Just where Nysa might have been.

Whether the two are related or not, that is, the birth of Dionysus and the origin of storage and transport technology invented by the Canaanites that would have carried wine to

new lands, in one way or another myth portrays the god of wine hailing from the ancient Near East, whether from Mesopotamia, Persia, Egypt, or Anatolia, the land of the ancient Hittites. Euripides works it out this way: Dionysus was indeed born in Thebes. Soon afterwards, however, he journeyed from Greece all the way to Arabia through Lydia and Phrygia (Anatolia-Turkey) and across Persia, Bactria, and Media (roughly Iraq, Iran, and Afghanistan), before returning once again to Greece. Given a certain liberty, the Arabia stopover of this Euripidean journey could loosely jive with the Homeric hymn's "part of Phoenicia."

Whatever the case, according to the different stories we have, the god seems to have been an outsider, an immigrant, we might even say an illegal alien, or, if we prefer, an undocumented worker of intoxicating miracles. In fact, Cadmus' conservative grandson Pentheus complains that Dionysus was "imported into Hellas." This was way back before imports were cool, during the days of "American only" goods. Consequently, he's for sending the dark haired god back over the border. At one point, a rather sour Pentheus complains about the frenzied and manic result of drinking wine, as though Dionysus' effect is the original reefer madness (doubtlessly brought by illegals). "Like a blazing fire this Bacchic violence spreads!"

Was Dionysus an import? Or was he born closer to home, as one early theory had it, that he came from Thrace and finally made his way down to Greece? This is the next question we'll briefly attempt to answer with the help of historians and archaeologists.

The earliest written evidence for Dionysus in Greece is inscribed in Linear B, the ancient syllabic writing system of the Mycenaean Greeks. The syllabograms *di-wo-nu-so-jo* are written on hundreds of clay tablets. Many scholars believe this refers to our god himself, Dionysus. The problem is the word or name could also simply denote any old bloke named Dionysus. So, they argue, the evidence is ultimately inconclusive.

What's certain is that Greeks were making wine as far back as four millennia ago if not earlier. Nevertheless, biomolecular archaeologists believe the impetus to ferment wine originated elsewhere than in ancient Hellas. Here's where the myths probably get the story right—at least loosely.

For its origins, we have to travel some eight thousand years back and thousands of miles east from Greece to the broad area of the Taurus Mountains in Turkey, the Caucasus in Georgia, and the northern Zagros Mountains in Iran. This is probably where wine originated. From there the divine beverage flowed down into Mesopotamia along the Tigris and Euphrates Rivers, over to the inhabitants of the Levantine coast, including the Ugaritic peoples, the Canaanites, and their foemen the Israelites, and down toward Egypt, which soon cultivated its own vines for wine along the Nile.

At this point, wine archeologists suggest that wine journeyed to Greece via two possible routes. One, the Phoenicians ferried it to the island of Crete in the middle of the Mediterranean, and from there, it made its way to the mainland. Two, other traders sailed it alongside the coast of Hittite Anatolia and into Greece through Thrace or the Aegean islands. Either way, the important point is that wine did indeed reach ancient Hellas. And for that, you and I thank the gods.

The Gift of Wine

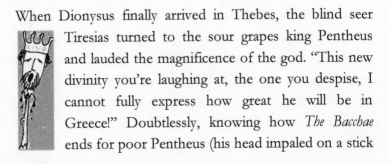

When Dionysus finally arrived in Thebes, the blind seer Tiresias turned to the sour grapes king Pentheus and lauded the magnificence of the god. "This new divinity you're laughing at, the one you despise, I cannot fully express how great he will be in Greece!" Doubtlessly, knowing how *The Bacchae* ends for poor Pentheus (his head impaled on a stick by his own mother), Dionysus will have the last laugh.

Tiresias goes on to enumerate the two chief gifts the gods have given to mortal men. As he does, the primordial teetotaler Pentheus stands by scoffing. The first gift is bread from Demeter, the earth and grain goddess. The other came when Dionysus,

> the son of Semele, discovered bread's counterpart, the drink that flows from the grape cluster. This he introduced to mortals. It is this that frees trouble-laden men from their pain—when they fill themselves with the juice of the vine— this that gives sleep to make a man forget the day's troubles. There is no other treatment for misery.

Tiresias finishes his encomium by declaring a significant aspect of the gift of wine, the fact that it is supposed to benefit both the gods and men. "Himself a god, he is poured out in libations [by humans] to the gods, and so it is because of him that men win blessings from the gods."

Later on, when a messenger arrives from Cithaeron, he confirms Tiresias' several points about Dionysus, while adding one more that is quite awesome. Pouty Pentheus listens, his arms folded in protest. "Whoever this god may be," declares the messenger, "welcome him to Thebes. For he is great in many other ways." He goes on to name wine's blessings. Aside from the usual alleviation of a man's suffering, Dionysus also helps with lovemaking and other pleasures. "If there is no god of wine, there is no love, no Aphrodite either, nor other pleasure left to men."

Wow, that's quite a statement of benefits. Wine is re- sponsible for both curing pain and for all the pleasures we humans know. Not bad, Dionysus Bro! The chorus leader Coryphaeus adds, "I tremble to speak the words of freedom before the tyrant [Pentheus]. But let the truth be told: there is no god greater than Dionysus."

Other early Greeks agreed. The epinician poet Pindar positively assesses wine as "the vine's potent child." The *Anacreontea*, a collection of poems in the style of those written by the larger than life hedonist Anacreon, adoringly terms wine "Dionysus' liquid harvest." The *Theogony* reports that Dionysus is "the dazzling and deathless god in whom many exult." Elsewhere, Hesiod refers to wine as "the gift of much-cheering [*polygēthēs*] Dionysus." Like Homer, who sings that the god is the *charma* or joy of mortals, so too does the *Shield of Herakles* designate wine a gift of the gods.

We'll learn much more about the positive uses, qualities, and effects of Dionysus' bequest in chapters 6 and 7. For now, let's finish with a delightful story from the seventh *Homeric Hymn to Dionysus*, which opens, "Of Dionysus, glorious Semele's son, I will make remembrance."

The story begins with the young god appearing on the seashore, his beautiful and wavy dark hair flowing and his purplish-red cloak flapping in the wind. Suddenly, freeboot-ers from Tuscany seize him, thinking he's "the son of a princely line," and that he'll fetch them a sizeable ransom. The problem is you can't bind the god of wine, something that vinegary Pentheus finds out the hard way in *The Bacchae*.

Well, once the men bring Dionysus aboard, the helms-man is terrified. "Madmen!" he cries out—using the word *daimonioi* that is doubtlessly a play on drunkenness. It means something like god-possessed. The helmsman rightly suspects they've kidnapped a god. He carries on, "This is either Zeus, or silver bow Apollo, or Poseidon; he's not like mortal men, but the gods who dwell on Olympus!"

How right he is!

As they sail on, the rest of the men ignoring the prudent helmsman, "they began to see miraculous apparitions." Here's the play by play of what they saw:

> At very first, wine bubbled up and out onto the dark swift ship, sweet-tasting and fragrant wine, followed by an ambrosial smell … Then along the very top of the sail there spread a twisting vine here and there, draped with many bunches of grapes. About the ship's mast, dark green ivy was twisting and spiraling upwards, flourishing with blossoms, and graceful fruit burst from the vine. Ivy wreathed all the thole pins.

Now the freebooting pirates are terrified! They desperately beg the helmsman to steer them ashore, but Dionysus prevents it. Unexpectedly, the god shape-shifts into a lion. Then he leaps at and seizes the captain of the ship who has foolishly supported the men against the helmsman. *Go Bro!* When the others see this, they fearfully leap into the sea to "avoid an evil fate." There they morph into happy dolphins—a good luck sign for Greek sailors. As for the helmsman, Dionysus turns to him and blesses him with all-happiness (*panolbios*).

The scene from the seventh *Homeric Hymn* is one we can readily imagine with the help of the *Dionysus Cup* (sometimes called the *Exekias Cup*) done by the mid-fifth century BC Athenian painter Exekias. Painted on the surface of the interior of a ceramic *kylix*, a large and shallow drinking cup, is a black-figure picture likely illustrating the hymn or a similar story. There, a crowned dark-bodied Dionysus reclines on a small ship, just as a Greek man might have reclined on a couch during a drinking party, a symposium.

The day is perfect. We can tell because a gentle breeze blows from behind the god filling the white sail before him. Around the black mast grows a vine, and from the deck and above the sail, it flourishes into a leafy gathering of twisted vines heavy with seven bursting grape clusters hanging down, pregnant with wine, waiting to shower the god with his own sweet liquid harvest. Around the ship, we see seven dolphins playfully swimming and jumping through the terracotta water. The Tuscan freebooters have indeed avoided a bad fate; they seem perfectly content, if not happy as dolphins (or maybe they're just drunk). Although Exekias didn't include the helmsman, we can imagine him reclining next to the god, pleasantly intoxicated with the divine beverage that erases all grief and brings happiness and love.

The helmsman is not the only one who is happy upon encountering Dionysus and imbibing wine. So too are all those men and women who partake of the Dionysian or Bacchic rites. These were part of a mystery religion celebrated in the ancient world for at least a thousand years. Among other elements, the religion included the nocturnal ritual of drinking wine with manic effect and eating raw flesh (omophagy) like an animal (think sushi). Early on in

The Bacchae, the chorus proclaims, "O blessed [*makar*] is the man who, happy [*eudaimōn*] in knowing the gods' rites … joins himself to the worshipful band, performing the Bacchic rites upon the mountains." It's a formula for happiness! Pindar likely echoes the recognition of this blessedness in a fragment of his we have: "Happy are all those with the good fortune of toil-relieving rites."

The chorus finishes by commanding, "On bacchants"—that's you, that's me. "On you bacchants! Bring the roaring son of a god, Dionysus, from Phrygia's mountains to Hellas' streets, broad for dancing!"

The story of Dionysus' kidnapping in the ship and the call to bring the roaring god into the towns and streets of Greece reminds you of the springtime festival celebrating the advent of Dionysus. During the celebration men wheel in a float-like boat with the god onboard as well as flowering vines and painted jugs of wine.

You close your eyes. You dream. You feel what will be the springtime breezes on your skin, imagine the drinking competition that you hope to win as your friends call out to you cheering you on, and recall the joyous fact that your youngest son will receive his first jar of wine next year at the sanctuary of Dionysus in the Marshes. He's only three.

Then you open your eyes. You're back on the ship rowing into Mytilene's busy port in Lesbos. Nemesis' hour has finally come! Soon the men of Mytilene will pay for their rebellion. When they do, the blood will flow like … well, you know.

It's now afternoon. You're in Mytilene, standing where the Mytilenian men usually gather when making a decision, like the one for rebellion they foolishly made some months ago. Gods help them.

As the trierarch reads the assembly's decision and mandate to the city's Athenian commander Paches, you wonder if there is presently a poet as great as Alcaeus was among the men alive today in Mytilene—one who can skillfully praise the god of wine as he did.

You dread what your own city has ordered. Soon, very soon, all the men will be dead and stacked in gruesome crimson corpse piles for burning in Hephaestus' fire. If there is such a poet, his talent will be wasted to satisfy Cleon's bloodlust.

But thank the gods, it never happens!

Instead, just after sending off the trireme with you and the others rowing to convey the deadly instructions to Paches, the remaining men of Athens relented and commissioned another ship to stop the murder.

"Quick!" they ordered. "Double time!"

They even supplied the new trireme and all the men onboard with extra wine and barley cakes to fuel the voyage night and day. There would be no slaughter.

Weeks pass by.

Now you're back on the trireme sailing home to Athens. Tired from the whole excursion and the long stay in Mytilene on Lesbos, you look forward to returning home. When you get to Athens, you plan to trek out to your farm some miles away from the Acropolis. There you'll tend your vineyard with your family and your few slaves. You'll walk down the path and see all the leafy green vines and foliage growing up around the vine poles, touch the soft, heart-shaped leaves notched all the way around, smell the soil from which the vines grow, pluck the dark grapes, and dream about the amphoras of wine they'll provide you, your family and friends for the days and months to come.

You hope your oldest son has taken due care while you've been gone. With that thought, however, you settle in to rowing at a relaxing pace. You know he has. You know because you're the one who taught him how to cultivate the vine.

Deliciously Fun Activity No. 2

Trace the origins, history, and distribution of your favorite wine

If you're like many of us oenophiles, you have a favorite wine that you drink repeatedly. It's your quotidian go-to for pleasure and positive satisfaction. But what do you know about your favorite wine?

Step one. Look into the origins of this wine. Where was it born? Not only in terms of the winery, region, state, or country, but what was the land like where it was grown and given birth? The earth, the soil, the vegetation, and climate? The *terroir*? What  about the land's people and music, literature and food?

What was the process of making the wine? What were the ingredients—the grape variety and otherwise? Who were the vintners at this winery (in essence, the Zeus and Semele of your favorite wine)?

Step two. What is the history of the winery where the wine was born? And what is the history of wine making in the local area, state, or country?

Step three. How did your wine reach you? If you ordered it online, who shipped it? If you bought it in a wine or liquor store, who distributes (and possibly imports) it to the store?

If you do this activity, I promise you'll appreciate your favorite wine even more.

Why? K = E. Knowledge equals enjoyment.

2

CULTIVATING THE VINE

A vine was luxuriant in the time of vintage with leaves and grapes. A Goat, passing by, nibbled its young tendrils and leaves. The Vine addressed him and said, 'Why do you thus injure me without a cause and crop my leaves? Is there no young grass left? But I shall not have to wait long for my just revenge; for if you now should crop my leaves and cut me down to my root, I shall provide the wine to pour over you when you are led as a victim to the sacrifice.'

—AESOP, THE VINE AND THE GOAT

THE TRIREME SAILS into the port of Athens, the Piraeus, roaring and weaving its way through the many other ships and smaller boats and finally into the naval dockyard.

When you disembark, you happen to meet up with an old friend who invites you to a reading of Homer by the professional rhapsode Ion. He's very popular right now throughout the whole of Hellas. A rhapsodic pop star.

Because it's already nearly sundown and you're bone tired from the toilsome journey, you agree. It'll be better to make your way to Athens and then on to your farm tomorrow. More, you'd like to hear Ion. He claims to know everything thanks to his knowledge of Homer.

Walking with your friend Cephalus to his house, you ask him what part of the poet the rhapsode will be singing, and more importantly, what kind of a party it will be—will the wine consumption be heavy or light? You pray heavy. Laughing, he declares the drinking will likely tend toward moderation since the so-called philosopher is also staying at his house. "Who do you mean?" you ask, though you suspect you already know. He nods when you guess Socrates. "Who else is coming?" The playwright Sophocles will be there too, he says, as well as Cephalus' own sons Lysias, Euthydemus, and Polemarchus, along with the sophist Thrasymachus (*O gods,* you think, *not him*), the tempestuous playboy Alcibiades, the staid physician Eryximachus, the businessman Callicles, and others. Then he tells you what part of Homer Ion will be performing.

Later on, with your desire for wine finally satisfied, Ion stands before you and a whole roomful of men and deftly recites from Homer's *Iliad* as if inspired by a god. There's

king Priam, he sings, standing next to the beautiful Greek woman Helen, whose abduction was the cause of the Trojan War. (All thanks to the men, of course.) Ion stretches his arms and hands out from the sides of his bone-white tunic and spreads them widely before going on.

Perched on a tower built high along the ashlar walls overlooking the dusty battlefield before Troy, Priam studies Agamemnon and the other Achaeans. Observing the great number of men the Achaean leader rules, he admiringly declares, "O blessed son of Atreus, offspring of Fate, prosperous-by-god. I see that the Achaeans are subject to you in great multitudes."

The sight below causes Priam to remember the time when he visited the kingdom of Phrygia in central Anatolia. "I once journeyed to the land of Phrygia, rich in vines," he says. He goes on to recall how many warriors the kingdom was able to employ against the Amazons, a reflection of the great number of vineyards they had for making wine. From his remark, it's clear he treasures fighting men and fertile vine land, as would have any proper Homeric hero.

The General Value of Vineyards

Ancient Greeks prized vineyards for two major reasons. Most obviously, vines were valued for their products—for the grapes enjoyed as sweet, juicy treats; for sugary raisins dried beneath the sun; and for fragrant wine, the natural but cultivated result of fermentation. Moreover, as with all farmland, vineyards served as a basis for wealth. As such, they indicated the extent of a man's rule. The man with more land typically dominated more men and women in terms of family and friends, servants and slaves. Because of this rule, the landowner had more power.

Predictably, then, Homeric Greeks were insistent upon handing all of this—the land, vineyards, rule, and power—over to the next generation. Odysseus alludes to this desire and the value of vine land for inheritance when, in order to identify himself, he reminds his father Laertes that he had once promised to give him a significant number of vinerows among other agricultural wealth (pear, apple, and fig trees).

"And rows of vines, too, you named to give me, fifty of them, which are ripe at separate times. And on the vines are bunches of grapes of all sorts."

From Odysseus' own testimony, we might conclude that his home island was a sufficiently decent if not a positively respectable place to cultivate the vine.

True, you think. But your own rich and valuable farmland just outside Athens is good as well. In your experience, your estate produces a strong and complex wine that stands up in competition to much of what you've tasted around Hellas, including Chian, Lesbian, Thasian, and Rhodian wine, not to mention the ancient vintage of Ithaca.

The fact that there are so many valuable vineyards covering Greece means that it's fair to declare the wine god has blessed you and the other Greeks. In gratitude, then, let's explore some of the vine lands mentioned by Homer.

Locating Vineyards

According to Athena disguised as a young shepherd, Odysseus' home island of Ithaca was actually more than merely decent for growing grapes. Although "it is a rough and rugged island, not fit for running horses because it is not wide enough," she judges, it is still not "yet utterly poor. Rather, in it grows an inexpressible amount of grain and grapes for making wine as well." Elsewhere, the goddess testifies that Ithaca's soil is *oinopedos*, wine-earth or wine-ground, that is, soil fit to produce vineyards and wine.

While Ithaca was good, many of the mythological lands mentioned by Homer in the *Odyssey* were apparently off the charts. Take the swineherd Eumaeus' childhood island of Syria (sometimes given as Syrie), where people neither get hungry nor grow sick. Among other positives, such as fertile land and ample herds, flocks, and wheat, Syria is "abounding in wine" (*oinoplēthēs*). It's full of the stuff! The land of the Phaeacians is similar. They were the people who last hosted Odysseus on his long and dangerous journey home and the ones who helped him reach Ithaca in their magical speedboats. Homer describes a luxuriant island replete with many kinds of fruit trees: pomegranate, pear, apple, fig, and olive trees that bloom the year around thanks to the weather blown in by the west wind. Such weather brings, "pears upon pears, apples upon apples, and grape bunches upon grape bunches." Similarly, the land of the Cyclopes is particularly rich, where there are "grapevines fostered by the rain storms of Zeus, which carry in them wine made of fine grapes."

Sailing away from these legendary lands located somewhere in the western Mediterranean (at least according to Ernle Bradford's adventurously fun book, *Ulysses Found*), if we boat to the Peloponnesian Peninsula where the Spartans lived, and speed our way overland by chariot as Odysseus' and Nestor's sons Telemachus and Pisistratus did, then we'll come to the far western side of the Peloponnese and to Epidaurus. This city was home to Asclepius' famous healing center, the *Asclepeion*. Homer tells us that Epidaurus was "rich in vines" or "vine clad" (*ampeloeis*, referring to vines twisting around the vine post). Doubtlessly, all the wine would have been important medicine for those seeking health during an overnight stay at Asclepius' colonnaded hospital shrine.

Well, if that doesn't work, we can always catch a merchant ship full of amphoras and slaves sailing up to Histiaea in northern Euboea or go further to Arne (aka Gla) in Boeotia. Homer names both towns as "rich in grapes" (*polustaphulos*, meaning 'many bunches of grapes'). On the other hand, if we're in the mood for a raid in imitation of the average Homeric hero who thrived on such rambunctious and daring activity, we can go further north to Thrace, to the land that is today northeastern Greece, southeastern Bulgaria, and the European part of Turkey. There we can sack a city following the lead of Odysseus and his men who sacked Ismarus, a town of the Cicones in Thrace. After they squashed all the men like a bunch of dark-skinned grapes and enslaved the women and children, they captured much booty, including a very fine and pleasant

wine (*methu hēdus*). According to Odysseus' testimony, "Each one of us drew a large quantity of wine into large two-handled jars when we seized the sacred citadel of the Cicones." I'll say more about this fine wine in Chapter 3.

Moving on, if we like to, we can depart from Thrace and sail some 70 miles due south to Lemnos, a fish-shaped island sacred to Hephaestus in the northern Aegean Sea. Although Homer doesn't describe Lemnian wine, we know that this volcanic island was a big producer and exporter of wine during the years of the Trojan War. Homer reports that "many ships carrying wine from Lemnos were anchored nearby" the Achaean encampment outside Troy.

Not far from their encampment, further on in Anatolia, Homer makes reference to three different lands that were particularly rich for farming and growing vineyards. In one instance, a surprised Achilles surmises the reason why the Trojan hero Aeneas is willing to challenge him in single combat. It has to do with this land. He figures Aeneas' side has promised Aeneas something really big. "Have the Trojans now apportioned a fine estate [*temenos*] for you, farmland standing out among other land, with vineyards and orchards [*phutalia*], and ploughland?" Two other times, and nearly word for word, Homer employs the same depiction of fine land to describe Bellerophon's and his grandson Sarpedon's land in Lycia in southwestern Anatolia.

Although much of Homeric and early Greece was good for growing vineyards and producing wine, a few islands were not, at least according to one myth and a popular proverb. In the *Homeric Hymn to Apollo*, Apollo's mother Leto asks the island Delos to host the birth of her son. If he does, she promises him fame and glory thanks to all the supplicants that will travel there to Apollo's shrine. If not he'll never amount to anything at all. Why? Because Delos is dry and barren, and so he'll never produce vineyards or other crops or foster bleating sheep. In the end, and knowing the stark truth of her evaluation, Delos agrees to the birth.

Sailing from Delos in the Cyclades, a circle of islands southeast of the mainland, if we cruise northeast toward Chios, we'll come to Psyra. It's a small island about fifteen miles west of Chios that inspired the saying, "Taking Dionysus to Psyra," thanks to the fact that it can't produce wine (it is treeless). Let me explain. According to a fragment we have from the choral poet Alcman of Sparta, if you were at a party in ancient Greece, and for whatever reason you didn't want to drink for the evening, you would say, "I'm taking Dionysus to Psyra." Put another way, you were making wine absent for yourself just as wine is absent from the island. For this reason, one scholiast or commentator on the *Odyssey* called Psyra a "wretched place." *Seriously*. I mean, why would anyone choose to take Dionysus to Psyra?

Doubtlessly, you agree as you sit there in Cephalus' large house in the Piraeus. By now, Ion has finished his theatrical recitation of Homer for the evening and you've retired to a room off the courtyard so that you can sleep early. You want to get up in the morning when the cock crows.

Lying there with your eyes closed, you hear the men talking loudly in the *andrōn* (the men's room). Above all, there's Thrasymachus (arggh!). Socrates has stirred them up about one matter or another. The last you heard, he was asking what Odysseus meant when he lamented hunger bidding a man by force to remember it. Did he mean that hunger and all other desires must necessarily be satisfied? You heard the businessman Callicles reply in the affirmative. "If a man wishes to be happy," he said. Thrasymachus heartily agreed.

Even though you're interested in what Socrates has to say—who isn't?—you're more eager to get a good night's rest in order to have ample vigor when you reach your farm toward mid-morning tomorrow. You have work to do. Moreover, you'll inevitably see him and the others again at a symposium in Athens. However much the man speaks of moderation, wherever there's a bowl of wine, there's Socrates.

The Typical Homeric and Early Greek Vineyard

As we see with the examples of Aeneas, Bellerophon, Sarpedon, and others such as Meleager who killed the monstrous Caledonian boar, Alcinous the Scherian king, and even the goddess Demeter, Homeric Greeks oftentimes divided off vineyards and other farmland into separate estates or official domains called pl. *temenē* (s. *temenos*).

Thanks to the mid-twentieth century scholarship of Oxford don Leonard Palmer and others, we may trace the word *temenos* back to Mycenaean times some three thousand years and more ago. At that time, the  term appears in several Linear B clay tablets found in the Archive Room at Pylos and at other Mycenaean citadels. From what scholars understand, *temenos* referred to land and agricultural products set apart for the *wanax* (king) or *lawagetas* (the leader of the war-host). It could also represent land reserved for or held sacred to a god or hero (as with Demeter above). In general, though, Homer uses *temenos* to identify an estate divided off and given to an individual man for his own use.

From the common language used by Homer and other early Greeks to describe vine land (for example, *polustaphulos* and *oinoplēthēs*) or land that was good for cultivating the vine (*oinopedos*), we can assume that most farms or *temenē* consisted of a large number of vinerows that produced many bunches of grapes. Even so, most farms were relatively small.

The famous shield of Achilles forged and crafted by the god Hephaestus gives us some idea of the organization and features of a typical Homeric vineyard. A farmer would  reach his vineyard by walking down a dirt footpath (*atrapos*), something doubtlessly created over time by natural wear and by purposefully clearing away brush and rocks. Once there, he would pass by a simple bridge over a ditch (*kapetos*) and walk through a gate in the stone wall (*herkos*) surrounding the vineyard. Presumably, the farmer intended the wall to keep out intruding animals and other humans.

Inside the wall, the farmer would see his beautiful vineyard (*alōē*) pregnant with grapes (*staphulē*). As the shield has it, the vineyard's grape bunches (*botrus*) are dark (*melas*) and honey-sweet (*meliēdēs*). The vines spiral up vine posts (*kamax*), their heart-shaped leaves spread out to create a measure of shade beneath the sun's summer rays. Here it is from the *Iliad*:

> On the shield, Hephaestus created a large vineyard pregnant with grape clusters, a vineyard beautiful and golden. And

dark were the grapes therein. The vines stood throughout
the vineyard on silver poles. And around the vineyard he
hammered a trench of dark-blue enamel as well as a wall of
tin. Beyond the wall, one single path led to the vineyard by
which the grape collectors came and went whenever they
gathered the fruit.

To imagine the vine poles, we can return once again to
the *Dionysus Cup* by Exekias. Recall, the god is reclining in a
ship that has suddenly sprouted a god-sized vine. The vine
itself twists around the mast as it would around a vine-prop.
This was the nature of the relationship between the pole
and vine. Like a twisting helix, the vine wraps itself around
the post until it reaches the upper part. I imagine this is why
Homer uses the word *ampeloeis* as shorthand to describe
"vine-clad" or "vine-wrapped" land. *Ampeloeis* comes from
two words, *amphi* (about, around) and *helix* (twisted, curved),
and signifies land full of twisting vines spiraling up around
vine trestles. In the *Dionysus Cup*, the flourishing leafy vine
twists and grows past the mast above the sail, where it
spreads out and hangs with seven dense bunches of grapes.

If we flip over to the end of the *Odyssey*, we'll find an
enlightening detail about how Homer's Greeks might have
made the vineyard's wall and of what material. There
Homer reports that when Odysseus went in search of his
servant Dolius, he, his sons, and other thralls were out
collecting stones for a wall. "He did not find Dolius when
he went down into the great orchard [*orchatos*], or any of his
sons nor the other slaves taken in war. Rather, they were
gone gathering stones for the vineyard wall." Given what
Athena and Homer say elsewhere about Ithaca, that it is

trachus (jagged and rough), I believe it is fair to assume that there would have been an ample supply of rocks and stones to collect for such a wall. Once gathered, these would have been stacked, one atop another, utilizing gravity to build up the wall.

Homer mentions similar vineyard features in a simile used to describe the battle fury and might of the Achaean warrior Diomedes as he attacks the Trojans in Book 5 of the *Iliad.*

> The hero rushed across the plain like a late winter river swollen by rain and snow that breaks up the dike with its flow—the dike piled high to defend against its attack. The mound does not confine or hold back its flow, however, nor do the walls of the luxuriant vineyard restrain the river's sudden coming when the heavy rain of Zeus falls in torrents. Rather, before it the many beautiful and strong works of men collapse.

There are two key aspects in Homer's description. One, there's the dike, or mound of earth (*gephura*), which was meant to protect the vineyard from flooding water toward the end of winter and beginning of spring. It is possible that ancient Greeks also built these to channel water for irrigation, but from what Homer alone details, we can't say.

Two, just as there are on Achilles' shield, so too does Homer mention walls (*herkos*) surrounding the vineyard. Although in this instance, the wall serves as a barrier to the rushing stream as it pours past the dike, the wall was likely meant for other security functions such as I mentioned before. You can still see these kinds of defensive stone barriers in Greece and Italy today.

The problem in Homer's simile is that neither the dike nor the wall protects against the heroic swollen river. Just as the Trojan army fails to hold back Diomedes, so too do they fail to do their proper work. A cold and stormy event like this would have been disastrous for a vineyard.

Fortunately, most Greek vineyards survived to produce their many grapes for wine. But first, you had to work long and hard to cultivate the plants and harvest the fruit.

Cultivating the Vine

The sun is burning high in the sky. It's just before noon and you've finally made your way up the three-mile long walled roadway from the Piraeus, through the bustling streets and marketplace of Athens, and out to your farm.

From the agora, you stroll up the Panathenaic Way, out the Dipylon gate, and through the shops where sweaty men sit making ceramic vessels of all kinds with terracotta and other potter's clay (*keramos*). After about the time it takes you to eat a small loaf of bread and drink a cup of wine, you turn right onto a small dirt trail leading to your farm that abuts the narrow Eridanos River. You can't wait to see how your oldest son and the servants have been tending the ploughland and vineyards since you've been gone. It's nearly been a month.

When you arrive, your wife happily greets you with a cold stew of boiled meat, vegetables, and barley, a slice of bread brushed with olive oil, raisins, and a cup of diluted wine. She tells you she's following the advice of Hippocrates, a travelling physician from the island of Kos, which leads you to roll your eyes when she's not looking.

"The goal of eating during the summer," she proclaims, "is to make the body cool and soft."

"Soft?" you ask.

"Wet," she responds.

You shrug and eat the stew and drink your wine. Whatever it's supposed to do, the food is tasty and the wine refreshing after your long hike from the Piraeus.

After a nap to avoid the heat of the afternoon, you make your way out of the farmhouse and down a hill to your vineyard. Walking along the path, you see the dike your father's father built up decades before to protect against the flooding Eridanos, and beyond that the more recent stone wall that defends your vines against intruders. It's not quite as tall as you are. Creeping above the wall, you spot the beautiful leafy green that indicates row after row of clustered vines. You notice a few slaves coming in and out through the wall's gate. And there's your oldest and most cherished son, working alongside them. You smile. The vineyard has come a long way since winter ended some six months ago.

Six months ago, you, your sons, and your slaves cut the vines in early spring. It's what you've done for as long as you can remember following the sage advice found in Hesiod's *Works and Days*. "When Zeus has completed sixty wintry days after the sun's solstice…"—that is, toward the end of February or beginning of March, when the star

Arcturus appears at dusk and swallows fly in the light—
"...then spring makes its stand once again, fighting off the
cold." The heroic farmer Hesiod's recommendation?
"Anticipate spring by pruning the vines first. For it is better
that way."

The first thing you do in the cycle of the year to care for
your vines, therefore, is to clip them in order to help them
properly grow and produce their fruit as the air turns warm,
the sun shines brightly, and the rains fall (sometimes).

The Greek verb Hesiod uses for clipping is *peritemnō*, the
same a physician such as Hippocrates would have used for
circumcision. But don't worry, as far as we know, plants
don't feel. And as far as the Greeks were concerned, we
know from Paul's famous fight with saints Peter and James
that Greek men were not typically cut in such a manner.
Only creeping plants with hanging grapes clusters were.

After trimming the vines, you work to clean up the
ground around each growing plant. Homer gives us some
idea of what this must have been like when Odysseus comes
upon his father toward the very end
of the *Odyssey*. He finds Laertes
cultivating the "well-built" (*euktimenos*)
vineyard, "digging around a vine
plant," fostering it with a small spade.
Seeing him, he praises his father for
his skill. "Old man, there is no
ignorance in your skill in tending well your orchards; rather,
your care is good. None of your plants lack proper attention, not the fig, olive, or pear trees, nor yet your vineyards."

Laertes smiles. He's proud of his work. Even so, Odysseus notices the shabby shape his father is in, a condition having to do with, among other things, the nature of the hard work it is to care well for an orchard and vineyard. Odysseus observes that the old man's tunic is dirty and tattered. Moreover, he's wearing soiled ox-hide greaves around his shins, patched gloves to protect his hands from brambles, thorns, and the prickly weeds that threaten the vines like a marauding army, and a roughly sewn goatskin cap to protect his venerable gray head from the sun.

Laertes is similar to the hardworking man in the fourth *Homeric Hymn to Hermes*. Walking through the countryside of grassy Onchestus in Boeotia, Hermes notices an "old man working on his blooming vineyard." He turns to him and declares, "Old man, hoeing around your vines with bent shoulders, you'll be rich in wine [*poluoineō*] when all these vines bear fruit."

I imagine the old man grinned, considering the many days he would be able to sit beneath the shade of a tree with his friends playing *pessos*, a checkers-like game, and drinking cup after cup of wine.

According to Hesiod, the work of hoeing and digging around the vines ends in mid-May, when the "house-carrier" the snail inches its way up from the dusty earth onto various plants. Then, he directs, "There is no longer any digging around the vines."

Rather, it is time to turn your attention to harvesting other crops. "Make haste," he advises, "and bring home the crops, getting up when the cock crows, so that the means of your life will be certain."

The vineyards must wait until late summer to give you their fruit.

Gathering Grapes and Making Wine

Four months have passed since you last fostered your vines and six since you pruned them. By now, all the stars have wheeled through the dark night sky so that presently Arcturus rises at dawn rather than at dusk as it did back in early March. According to Hesiod, it is mid-September and time to collect the grapes. "When Orion and Sirius travel into the middle of the heavens, and rosy-fingered Dawn sees Arcturus, then, Perses, harvest all the grapes and take them home."

How will you gather the grapes? The pseudo-Hesiodic poem the *Shield of Heracles* suggests that farmers collect the grapes by means of a reaping hook or sickle (*drepanē*). Describing the work taking place along the surface of the "divine earth," the plowing and reaping of wheat, pseudo-Hesiod reports that "others were gathering grapes from the vines, holding reaping hooks in their hands." From there the happy reapers (doubtlessly grim to the poor grapes) haul the precious fruit to woven baskets (*talaros*) lined up along the vineyard's edge. "Others were carrying white and black grape clusters from the gatherers to wicker baskets, from the big rows of vines."

While some work to collect the grapes and others toil to plow the field and harvest the grain, there are a few men present to provide entertainment and refreshment. The *Shield* tells us that pipe players pipe cheerful tunes to motivate the workers. Otherwise, Homer hints at the fact that there is a good deal of drinking on the job. (So much for drug and alcohol testing in the workplace.) In the *Iliad*, we find the following delightfully unexpected description of an agricultural scene on Achilles' shield:

> Hephaestus wrought also a fair fallow field, large and three times plowed already. Many men were working at the plow within it, turning their oxen forward and backward, furrow after furrow. Each time they turned upon reaching the end of the row, a man would come up to them and give them a cup of honey-sweet wine, and they would go back to their furrows looking forward to the time when they would once again reach the end.

Imagine that! Every time you finish a report or make a sale, you get a cup of wine. Here Larry, try this Petite Syrah. Have a Chardonnay, Susan. Thanks, John.

I'm afraid that if this were the case today, far more of us would be in AA. Back in the day, though, when you and your children and slaves worked your vineyards on your farm outside Athens, it wasn't an issue. In fact, all of you drink early and much throughout the day and all your (relatively) short lives.

Which brings us to the point we've all been waiting for. Let's make some wine!

After we pluck the grapes and fill the wicker baskets, the *Shield* relates that the gatherers then carry them to others who will make the wine. For the next steps, Hesiod gives us the best instructions, though we'll also hear from Homer.

To begin with, Hesiod directs us "to bring the grapes out under the sun for ten days and ten nights." Next, he advises us to cover the grapes in shade for another five days. On the sixth day following that—the sixteenth in—he gives us the order that we've salivated over for nights on end: "Draw out the gift of much-cheering Dionysus into storage vessels."

But wait, you say. What about treading the grapes? You know, the whole practice that encourages the sugary insides to mix with the fruit's yeasty skin to begin the fermentation process. Haven't you ever seen that hilarious scene from the old sitcom *I Love Lucy*, where a very delicate Lucy, who has feet "like large pizzas," and a plump Italian lady, who has eaten an untold number of pizzas, get into a sloppy brawl that ends with them wrestling in the grape must? (Or am I just dating myself? It was a rerun, I promise!)

Well, interestingly, Hesiod doesn't mention anything about treading (*trapeō*) the grapes. Fortunately, Homer does in reporting on the activity of the Phaeacians. Singing of their grape growing and wine making operation, Homer explains that while some Phaeacian men are gathering grapes, "others are treading them."

To finish the process, we have to return to the *Shield of Heracles*. After the gatherers collect the grapes and pile them into the wicker baskets, the *Shield* informs us that "while some men were treading grapes, others were drawing off the juice" for making wine. *Thank the gods!*

What a delight! With Homer, Hesiod, and the *Shield*, we get the complete ancient Greek wine making process from beginning to end, from gathering the grapes into baskets, to treading them into must, and finally, to drawing off the juice or wine into jars.

So, when is it best to enjoy the wine we've made?

Your oldest son looks at you like your asking him something meant to trick him. Everyone knows the answer to that question. Quoting Hesiod, he clarifies that although the "new wine" comes in the fall before winter, "the wine is best" in mid-July.

True, you think. How true.

With a grin, you invite your son to come along and enjoy a cup of wine with you.

As the two of you walk up to the house, you describe the new wine cups you bought in Mytilene. You can't wait to serve wine in them, you say.

"Did you buy any wine while you were there?"

You nod. Not much, but enough.

Merchants there were offering Lesbian wine at a discount in celebration of the fact that there was no slaughter. Since the blood didn't flow, the wine did. At least that's what they called out as they hawked the wine.

Deliciously Fun Activity No. 3

Grow a backyard vineyard or *visit and work at a local vineyard*

Most of us can grow a small grapevine in our backyards, even those of us who live in relatively extreme environments. So try it. All you need is soil that drains well, circulating air, and sufficient sunshine. You can even do it in a pot or a barrel (think of it!).

The following are a few of the more useful websites and links I've found online for growing backyard vines:*

▪ *Grape Growing Guide* (www.grapegrowingguide.com): this easy to navigate site will help you start your vineyard, train and prune your vines, control pests, and make your wine.

▪ *How to Grow Stuff* (www.howtogrowstuff.com): this all-around gardening site has a vineyard growing page that's detailed and easy to follow.

▪ *Backyard Fruit Nursery* (www.backyardfruit.com): this website for the backyard gardener is a general spot for fruit, grape, and other nursery related products.

▪ For help on making your own wine, go to these fine websites: *How to Make Homemade Wine* or *Easy-Wine* (www.howtomakehomemadewine.com or www.easy-wine.net).

You may also want to try the following books:

- *From Vines to Wines: The Complete Guide to Growing Grapes and Making Your Own Wine* (Jeff Cox, Storey Publishing)
- *Grape Growers Handbook* (Ted Goldammer, Apex Publishers)
- If organic is your thing—and mother Gaia strongly suggests it—then check out *The Organic Backyard Vineyard: A Step-by-Step Guide to Growing Your Own Grapes* (Tom Powers, Timber Press)

If for some reason you don't want to experiment with the gift of Dionysus in your own backyard, then visit a local vineyard—most states have them (even Alaska!)—and ask for a guided tour.

Some vineyards will even let you help in the pruning, gathering, or wine making process. I know of vineyards where I live in Texas, for example, that have "pruning parties" (aka "circumcision celebrations") in the first few months of each year.

- To find wineries throughout the United States, go to *All American Wineries, LLC*—an online Winery and Vineyard Guide by State (www.allamericanwineries.com).
- For wineries and wine related events in cities in the U.S. and around the world, click on the "City Index" tab under "Events" at *Local Wine Events* (www.localwineevents.com).

* Unfortunately, due to the fluid nature of the World Wide Web and the publishing industry, the above resources may have changed location or availability since publishing *Drinking Wine*. If so, my apologies. Otherwise, I should note that I am not associated with nor do I profit from any of the above!

3

ANCIENT GREEK WINES

Hecamede, who is like a goddess, mixed for them a divine drink made with Pramnian wine ... and when they drank it, the mixture satisfied their intense thirst for a drink.

—HOMER, THE *ILIAD*

YOU AND YOUR OLDEST son amble up to the farmhouse discussing the best way to train vines to creep along the trellis. You're in no hurry.

You share with him an opinion you once heard from a very old man from Croton in southern Italy who had known and followed the mathematician and mystic Pythagoras before he died. Since then, you've taken the view on as your own, even though you're not nearly as certain as the old man was. Vines have a mind of their own, you explain, even as men do in their chests and heads. The bright green leaves turn this way and that, greeting Helios when he rises in the morning and following him all day long as he rides across the sky. The leaves are the many heads of the vine. How else is it possible for them to behave this way, you ask, except the vines employ some kind of intelligence and wisdom?

Your son shrugs and wisely admits the possibility, adding that the vine's intelligence might simply be an extension of Mother Earth's own intelligent activity.

When you reach the house, you go to the back and to the dugout clay-brick cellar where you keep your wine. There, just as in Odysseus' storeroom and in the cave of the immortals Hermes and Maia, you delight in the number of wine jars you have on hand. Three of them are from Lesbos, the wine you bought when you were in Mytilene just three days ago. You happily point out the official Lesbian stamp bearing Cybele on both handles of each amphora. Your son says something like, "Cool!" which makes you feel good—a bit younger than you are.

Calling a servant to the storeroom to help, you loosen the seal and lid on one of the amphoras of Lesbian wine. As you do, a fragrant smell rises to greet you and your son. You order the servant to ladle out a small, unmixed sample and it meets every expectation. *Gods!*

Although your own vineyard produces an excellent pour, and you have access to many quality wines in Athens and the Piraeus, you thoroughly enjoy tasting different wines from all over Hellas and wherever else Greeks live in Persia, Egypt, Libya, Italy, and further west toward the Gates of Heracles.

Wines, *Kykeōn*, Grog, and Nectar

We've now seen that Homeric Greeks grew vineyards and produced wine in every corner of ancient Greece, from Odysseus' home island of Ithaca in the west, to the land of the Cicones in Thrace in the north, and to Phrygia and Lydia in the eastern lands allied with Troy.

Our next goal is to explore what varieties of wines they produced. How did these taste, and what language did ancient Greeks use to describe their wine?

Although we don't know what the heroes called the many varieties produced by just as many vineyards in Homer's world, we can assume that each of them was unique given the slight variations in *terroir*—soil, climate, and other factors. Consequently, whether it was Lesbian wine, as you've bought, or a Chian vintage from the island of Chios, like that which the poet Ion supplied the Athenians when he gloriously won a contest in Attica, each wine had its own distinctive character even as wines do today.

The entertaining authors of *Divine Vintage: Following the Wine Trail from Genesis to the Modern Age* list many ancient prized wines. There were white, salt-watered wines from Kos; apple perfumed Thasian wines; a light and sweet wine from Knidos; another salted Rhodian wine; and Mesogitan wines from Magnesia and Ephesus in Anatolia. Then there were a variety of medicinal wines, including an ancient laxative from Cilicia along the southern coast of Turkey. (Or was this just your grandfather's prune juice?)

Unfortunately, aside from locations where they grew vineyards, we don't know much about the specific wines Homeric Greeks were drinking. Luckily, however, Homer does refer to at least two. I'll get to these in a moment.

For now, I want to explore the wine Hesiod names in the *Works and Days* when he kindly recommends an afternoon of relaxation and drinking to his bro Perses. He urges him to sit beneath the shadow of a rock overhang or a tree and invites him to chill with a jug of Bibline (aka Bybline) wine.

Doubtlessly, Perses heartily thanks Hesiod for such a stress-relieving suggestion, since his hard-ass brother has been working his tail off for the past year. (It's the only way to get ahead and make your neighbors jealous, says Hesiod.) He's had his poor bro busy preparing, plowing, planting, pruning, picking, and superstitiously praying to the gods, not to mention pissing in the right place (*not* into holy streams) and in the best direction (facing away from the sacred Sun). It's all been enough to make Perses, whose name means something related to the verb for sacking a city (*perthô*), want to go back to the life of a plundering pirate.

On second thought, maybe he could just find another job, a mudbrick apartment, and a girlfriend in Byblos, the Near Eastern home of Bibline wine in modern Lebanon. If he did make the move, it would take him to a very ancient Canaanite, then Phoenician, city, before the Assyrians conquered it just prior to when Perses would have arrived toward the end of the seven hundreds BC.

At any rate, Bibline wine had quite the stellar reputation in the ancient world. The wine archeologist and historian god Patrick E. McGovern reports that later Greek writers list it as "fine and fragrant" and the "equal of the best Greek wine from Lesbos"—of which I'll say something more in a moment.

Was Hesiod's Bibline wine imported from Byblos in Phoenicia? Yes and no. By yes, I mean that the Phoenicians probably shipped and transplanted Bibline vines to Thrace.

If true, then Thrace was likely the source of Hesiod's go-to "Bibline" wine. Knowing this source raises an interesting possibility.

Just over a third of the way through the *Odyssey*, the hero Odysseus brags about an exceptional wine that he and his comrades received from Maro, the son of Evanthes. When I say, "received," I mean it in the same way that a Mafioso collects payments to defend and protect various clients. Put another way, Maro paid off Odysseus and his men with twelve jars of this Ciconian wine to save his own skin when they sacked Ismarus, the city of the Cicones, where he lived in a wooded grove sacred to Apollo. According to the godfather Odysseus, they protected Maro and his family "out of reverence." Sure, Odysseus, just as Don Carlo protects the local pizza shop owner because he has a picture of the pope and Our Lady of Loreto.

Now, the Cicones were not Greek. Instead, they were a Thracian tribe that lived just north of Greece (if you were an Athenian snob) or in northern Greece (if you were a Macedonian or northern Greek wannabe). Regardless, the significance of their being Thracian means this: Depending on when the Phoenicians transplanted those Bibline vines from Byblos, the Ciconian wine could have been Bibline wine!

Either way, Odysseus proffers many details about the Thracian wine. In terms of type, it was a red (*eruthros*) wine that was very dark (*melanos*). To taste, it was pleasant (*hēdus*) and honey-sweet (*meliēdēs*). The Cyclops Polyphemus compares the wine to a distillation of nectar and ambrosia. Given the fact that Ibycus of Rhegium tells us that ambrosia and nectar are nine times as sweet as honey, this Ciconian wine was very sweet indeed. Then again, it could have been ultra-sweet because Polyphemus tossed it back unmixed (*akērasios*), which means it was very strong, and, therefore, whatever sweetness it had was intensified many times over. Odysseus reports that when consumed, it was usually first blended with twenty measures of water, resulting in a ratio of one part wine to twenty parts water. It's a remarkable ratio considering the usual wine to water ratios expressed in ancient Greek literature. Hesiod advises one to three, for instance.

Aside from this Ciconian-Thracian wine, Pramnian wine is the other wine named in Homer. It shows up in both the *Iliad* and the *Odyssey*. Sadly, neither instance sheds light on what the wine was like for Homeric Greeks.

To find out what this wine from the island of Lesbos was like, we have to rely on modern oenologists. Some tell us it was likely a muscat-based wine, sweet to the taste. Others believe it was an herbal wine. Either way, Pramnian wine was popular in Homer as the base liquid for one of the world's first mixed drinks (as least as we find them in literature).

Whether it means anything or not, females always mix the drinks in Homer—stirred not shaken. By females, I mean both mortal women and immortal goddesses. First, we witness Nestor's beautiful prize woman from Tenedos Hecamede mix him and his male guests a mixture of Pramnian wine, grated feta  cheese, and white barley. Some suggest she must have added honey to the *kykeōn* (mixed drink). It's possible, but impossible to confirm, as Homer doesn't say. Homer does nevertheless mention the fact that when Hecamede sat them down in Nestor's hut on chairs, she served them onions, barley meal, and honey as a relish for their drink. So perhaps honey did make it into the *kykeōn* after all.

Aside from the mortal Hecamede, the goddess Circe serves Odysseus' men the same mixed drink, with the small addition of a *pharmakon* (drug) that turned them into pigs. Sorry, guys. Fortunately, Odysseus was absent at the initial offering, and so he was able to swing into action with the help of Hermes, reversing the drug's effect before trapping and making love to Circe (she was a looker, just like all of James Bond's women are).

This Pramnian-cheese-barley-honey mixed drink is similar to early alcoholic beverages made in Greece going back some four thousand and more years. Patrick McGovern calls these "grogs." In short, they were fermented drinks made from a sundry of ingredients. Later, participants in the Eleusinian mysteries used similar drinks in their religious rituals. The mixture (*kykeōn*) shows up in the second *Homeric Hymn to Demeter*, where Metanira makes it for Demeter who is searching for her lost daughter Persephone. McGovern argues that in the end, these Bronze Age grogs ultimately lost out to wine brought over to Greece by the Phoenicians.

You may be wondering if beer ever shows up in Homer. The short answer is no. Although Herodotus much later mentions the Egyptian predilection for beer, and Archilochus of Paros, who lived just after the *Iliad* and *Odyssey* were first written down, sings about Thracians and Phrygians sucking *brutos* or barley-wine through a tube (*aulos*), there's no evidence in Homer for Bud-like barley-water.

What does show up is heavenly nectar, the drink of the everlasting gods. Like human wine, nectar is red (*eruthros*) and sweet (*glukus*). But don't forget, nectar (as well as ambrosia) is nine times sweeter than honey; therefore, it is far sweeter than any human wine.

Part of the sense of nectar's sweetness may be metaphorical. The reason is because nectar helps the gods live forever, which is pretty sweet—unless, of course, you happen to be Tithonus, who was granted everlasting life without agelessness, meaning he grew older without ever dying. The word nectar itself comes from the words *nek* (death, as in necropolis, a cemetery or city of the dead) and *tar* (overcoming). It thus means 'overcoming death.'

Part of nectar's life-granting quality comes from its ability to strengthen and sate all thirst. But more. Since the gods neither eat bread nor drink wine, they do not have blood, that is, human blood. Instead, they have immortal blood or divine ichor. Just as humans maintain their mortal blood by bread and wine, so too do the immortals sustain their ichor by nectar and ambrosia.

This means that if you are a god, you never *ever* want to go without nectar, as will happen if you falsely swear an oath by the river Styx—this according to Hesiod's *Theogony*. If you swear such an oath, the penalty is that you have to go without nectar and ambrosia for a whole year! (*My gods!*)

Conversely, if you are a god or goddess in Hades, as Persephone was while her poor mother was searching for her, then you should go on a nectar fast, as is only fitting.

Immortal nectar isn't exactly an appropriate drink for the realm of the dead. No, in the Underworld, the dead drink mud milkshakes and eat mud pies—at least if the *Epic of Gilgamesh* from ancient Mesopotamia has anything to say.

One last point about nectar. It comes to us once again straight from Hesiod's own mouth in the *Theogony*. Nectar was the beverage that helped the gods of Zeus' generation and their allies, namely Briareus, Kottos, and Gyges, to defeat the older generation of gods. When they downed the nectar, they were able to shoulder the machine-gun like boulder thrower that destroyed the Titans and tossed them nine to ten days and some thirty thousand miles down to dark Tartaros.

Incidentally, the author of the New Testament's Second Letter of Peter tells us that God sent the sinful angels (demons) to Tartaros, "putting them into gloomy dungeons to be held for judgment." This inspired revelation naturally causes me wonder: are angels just Titans? Better yet, perhaps after we have a few cups of conversation-promoting, speculation-rousing Lesbian wine while watching the "History" channel, we'll realize they are merely ancient aliens! It's funny how one word can raise so many possibilities.

Language Describing Wine

Speaking of words, let's move on. One of Homer's favorite words for wine is "honey-sweet" (*meliēdēs*). Relative to the liquid of the vine, the adjective could mean a few things. Most obviously, it signifies a very sugary wine sweetened with honey. Otherwise, *meliēdēs* could simply point to the quality that grapes naturally have, as Homer also uses the word for fruit in general.

On the other hand, since the term is used for life (honey-sweet life) and sleep, which sweetly takes away one's  concerns and anxieties, honey-sweet is also likely intended to refer to wine's ability to relieve anxiety. Along these same lines, Homer calls wine *meliphrōn* (sweet to the mind, delicious) from *meli* (honey) and *phrēn* (midriff, heart—the location of the spirit or mind).

It's clear from these adjectives that Homer's Greeks prized sweet wine. (I don't know if I could have lived back then. I mean occasionally I like some sweet Dionysus, but always?) Perhaps they desperately needed all the mellifluousness to offset all the bitter anger and grim warfare in their lives. Regardless, "sweet, pleasant" (*hēdus*) was another word employed to indicate a good wine (seen as well in *meliēdēs*).

In short, the model Homeric equation seems to have been GW = SW (good wine equals sweet wine). Good wine was "sweet to drink" (*hēdupotos*). And truly off-the-charts, heavenly wine, i.e. nectar, was *glukus*, to which our own English word glucose is a cousin.

The best wine, that which was "much asked for, choice, or excellent" (*exaitos*)—Robert Fagles translates it "the finest stock"—was *theios*, "of the gods, divine, wondrous." We might even say that *the* god Zeus himself hallowed it from on high, raining down his blessings on the vines as the Cyclops Polyphemus indicates. "For among the Cyclopes, the earth … bears fine grape clusters of wine, and the storms of Zeus give increase to them." Whatever role Zeus played, the fact that there were choice wines indicates that there was a hierarchy of wines in Homer's world.

Then, like now, a truly fine wine was old in years (*palaios*). When Telemachus goes down to the storeroom in his father's house, he observes all the *palaios* wine in large jars that Odysseus hoped to return to and enjoy after the Trojan War. Aside from this old wine, Homer mentions eleven year-old (*hendekatos*) wine that Nestor serves to his newly arrived guest Telemachus. Not bad.

Doubtlessly, when Nestor's servant uncovers the wine, draws some of the unmixed (*akratos*) liquid out, mixes it with water, and serves it, the wine is *aithops* (shining or sparkling, a word also used of bronze glimmering in the sun). I say doubtlessly, because aside from *meliēdēs*, *aithops* is Homer's go-to word for wine.

When Telemachus drinks the *eruthros* (red or ruddy) eleven year-old wine, he feels that warm feeling that arrives just after one imbibes. It's that happy feeling that makes you declare that wine is *euēnōr*, the joy of man, glorious, a man-exalter. And the cheer makes you wish to see wine (*oinos*) everywhere.

So it is that Homer describes the sea (mostly) and cattle (less so) as wine-colored or wine-faced (*oinops*) nearly thirty times in his epics. For example, "Agamemnon gave the Arcadian warriors benched ships with which to sail over the wine-colored sea."

Given such abundant wine-fuelled sweetness, joy, and cheer, we may happily hymn Dionysus before we tip back our cups of Lesbian wine. Indeed, we must!

> Be gracious, Bull god, you who drive women mad with sweet delight! Rejoice, fair-eyed child of Semele, you who inspire sweet song and divine singing! O Dionysus of the many grape clusters, grant us joyful pleasure again and yet again, season after season!
>
> —*Lines combined from Homeric Hymns 1 and 26 to Dionysus*

And the congregation calls out, *Amen, brother!*

And Perses bids farewell to his own brother Hesiod as he takes a ship to Byblos in Phoenicia in order to find a new master, a new job, and hopefully a new woman to love in a domestic nest of family tenderness and flowing wine (not necessarily in that order). (By the way, this is just my fantasy for him—in reality, we don't know what happened to Perses.)

As for you and your oldest son, you shout out to the original Bro Dionysus while standing next to the jar of Lesbian wine in your cellar.

The servant prepares to draw out a jug for you. Your mouth waters and the neurons of your brain fire (even though you don't know it).

Deliciously Fun Activity No. 4

Try a new wine or wine-like beverage

Many of the wines we drink today are aged in costly small oak barrels (or if you're drinking a wine from Australia, it may have been similarly seasoned with oak chips or sawdust). What this means is that whether we're drinking a Merlot or a Cabernet Sauvignon, a Shiraz or a Pinot Noir, the same underlying oaky flavor is there. They all taste similar!

Don't get me wrong—this is a good thing. I love the stuff! (Except I don't like thinking about oak in terms of sawdust. Why? It reminds me of eighth grade gym class and square dancing with Gretchen F.—though that's not the problem. Rather, this is: I later invited her to the sock hop. That she said 'yes' was divine—I thanked Aphrodite—as was the slow dance to REO Speedwagon's "Can't Fight This Feeling" and the craziness of Van Halen's "Jump." No, all was well until she told me she just wanted to be friends after the dance, when I was preparing to… Then "friend" became a four-letter word to me—as the band Cake sings on *Fashion Nugget*. And so that's what I think of when I hear the word sawdust. Oak barrels, yes; oak chips, sure; oak sawdust, hades no!)

The point: go out of your way to experience a wine that's different from your usual familiarity and routine. A different grape or fruit. Perhaps even mead (a honey-based beverage; some think nectar was mead). A different region and *terroir*. A different method of aging. And if you have a Gretchen in your life, a different friend, one that accepts you for who you are (I've long forgiven her).

Most importantly, try wines from different areas of the ancient Greek world, from southern Italy (what the Greeks called Magna Graecia) to Greece itself and its many wine-producing regions.

A useful book in this regard (one exploring wines around the world, including Italy and Greece) is Roger Barlow and Mark Rowlinson's *101 Wine Regions: A Tour of the Best and Most Uplifting Wine Regions in the World* (Parragon).

Happy drinking!

4

TRADING DIONYSUS' GIFT

From these ships, the Achaeans bartered for their wine, some with bronze, some with iron, some with hides, some with cattle, and some again with captive slaves taken in war.

—HOMER, THE *ILIAD*

WHEN YOUR SERVANT reseals the wine jar after ladling out a small jug of wine for you and your son to share, you tell your son that someday he may also go to Lesbos as you recently did.

You hope not, of course, at least not under the same circumstances that compelled you to go. But soon your son will be fighting for Athens, so unless the already half decade long war with Sparta ends quickly, then ... gods, you don't even want to think about it! Although you've had your share of fighting in the front lines and maneuvering at sea, it petrifies you to imagine him in the same situation facing similar dangers.

Your son asks you what Mytilene was like, and you describe the city with its market, slipping into the mode of a dull but informative pedagogue.

The home of Pittacus, one of the seven wise men of Ancient Greece, Mytilene has been a center of trade and manufactures for centuries. There are two harbors, one north and one south of the city. Around these, freemen and slaves alike work to make vessels of bronze and iron, beautifully dyed cloth, and painted pottery and clay figurines. Some of these—statues of Cybele, Isis, Aphrodite, and Eros—are worshipped in the temple of Demeter in the Acropolis. The Mytilenians export the rest to Greek cities throughout the Aegean along with Lesbian wine and other products.

You ask your son if he recalls the line by the poetess Sappho bidding her daughter Cleis to be satisfied with a local Mytilenian headband (*boring*, Mater) rather than one from Sardis in Lydia (that all the cool girls were wearing).

He does remember it.

Well, you go on, Sappho references things like these headbands from all over the Aegean, from Geraestus in Euboea, to Phocaea in Ionia, to Gryneia in Aeolia.

What she doesn't mention is the fact that the city transacts business with the whole world. Think about that!

Your son grows wide-eyed and you can tell he would like to go there someday—*everywhere*.

The old man Herodotus has, and he's told you about it. Ships sail to Mytilene from all the Greek trading cities west and east, as well as from non-Greek cities.

Trade is booming, you say. It always has been, and you presume it always will thrive just as it does now in the Piraeus and Athens and other major trading cities.

Early Trade

By the time of the Peloponnesian War (431-404 BC), Greeks had been plying the sea and trading for at least a thousand years going back to the Mycenaean Greeks, who dominated the mainland, Crete, and other islands during the last half of the second millennium BC.

Given what we know about them—the Linear B records the Mycenaeans maintained on clay tablets, the storage rooms they stocked full of wine jars and other goods, and their manufactures discovered throughout the Mediterranean (most notably, fine pottery)—Mycenaean Greeks traded extensively with many empires, kingdoms, and smaller city-states during the second millennium BC. The Canaanites of the Levantine coast were one important trading partner, at least in terms of the exchange of wine. Later on, the Canaanites now Phoenicians dominated sea trade during the Dark Ages of Greece.

Once the Dark Age period of economic and cultural stagnation ended, however, the Greeks aggressively began to imitate the Canaanite-Phoenicians in terms of trade, their alphabet, and wine culture. Finally, the Greeks operated everywhere, simultaneously establishing and strengthening colonies around the Mediterranean. By the time we get to Homer and Hesiod in the late seven hundreds BC and in the years following, there were Greek colonies or trading posts in modern France, Libya, Egypt, Syria, and around the Black Sea. For ancient Greeks, this was the whole world. And like the arteries and veins that run throughout your body carrying its life blood to every part, Greeks, Phoenicians, and others were transporting wine to every area of the world so that men and women everywhere could live normal, healthy, god-blessed lives.

Trade in Homer and Hesiod

Generally speaking, there were four major ways to produce and obtain desirables and other wealth in Homer's world: farming and local production; gift exchange within the context of a guest-host relationship; raiding and plundering; and lastly, trade.

If you were part of the Homeric nobility, you happily condoned the first, especially if your slaves were the ones working; the second, particularly if you were on the receiving end; and the third whenever you got the chance. But when it came to the fourth, you would raise a critical eyebrow at the mention of trade.

Nevertheless, to some extent in the *Iliad*, and far more in the *Odyssey*, trade is ubiquitous, however ambiguous its status was among the elite hero class.

We catch a glimpse of this ambiguity, nay antagonistic aversion, when the otherwise polite Phaeacian hero Euryalos insults Odysseus by calling him a—prepare yourself for this—a TRADER.

(My gods!)

Euryalos' heavy-duty accusation: "I suppose you are one of those grasping traders that go about in ships as captains or merchants, and who think of nothing but their outward freights and homeward cargoes." In other words, all you think about is profit—you Adam Smith loving, portable

Wealth of Nations carrying, green underwear sporting capital-ist!

He finishes by informing Odysseus that he's no athlete.

What? cries Odysseus. *Nooo—!*

You can imagine that our hero is pissed! Rising up, Odysseus throws off his cloak, revealing an **A** for athlete tattooed on his waxed chest, and hurls a discus farther than any one man of the Phaeacians could throw.

See, he finishes, pounding his chest, *I'm no trader!*

In the end, Euryalos apologizes, making up for his identification error with the guest gift of a sword.

Apparently, Homer's heroes were comfortable with augmenting their wealth by means of exchanging gifts; trading for profit, however, was not something a gentleman hero would do.

As I've already generally noted, the Phoenicians fully embraced a life of trading. This was true not only historical-ly, but in Homer too. It was Phoenician traders and slave dealers, for instance, that took a young Eumaeus from his home island of Syria and sold him into slavery.

When the swineherd Eumaeus relates the event, he ex-plains that the Phoenicians were "cunning traders, men famed for their ships, greedy knaves, bringing countless beautiful objects for trade in their black ship." When they came to his own homeland to trade, "The Phoenicians stayed a whole year until they had loaded their ship with much precious merchandise."

Odysseus backs up the swineherd's account, albeit with a lie. Fibbing to Athena, he claims to have travelled with the Phoenicians on one of their merchant tours. Interestingly, he describes a clockwise journey from Crete to Pylos or Elis, rather than the counterclockwise Mediterranean trading circuit typically given by modern historians. Another of his stories describes a similar clockwise route from the Levantine coast to Libya, when a Phoenician man, "a greedy knave"—there's that heroic bias against trading again—talked him into "conveying a cargo with him" to North Africa. In the end, the acquisitive man hoped to sell Odysseus into slavery.

Hesiod wasn't too big on trade either. In a dreamy disquisition on what I call the City of Justice, the city that naturally "blooms as the people flourish," he claims that the earth bears sufficient grain, grapes, and woolly sheep for the city's fortunate citizens so that they have no need to sail abroad to trade. It's Pangloss' best of all possible worlds.

Trading, after all, is an unnecessary risk born of needless longing that seizes you and bids you sail the stormy seas. Asserts Hesiod. No, if you work hard enough and seek justice, my brother Perses, you'll have no need to go gallivanting around, even if it's in search of a good job, a good wine, or a good woman.

Then the truth comes out. In an hour-long session with his therapist, we come to understand why Hesiod truly doesn't like sailing and trading abroad. He's got serious issues

with his father—perhaps some kind of a Kronos fixation (recall: Kronos lopped off his father's penis in Hesiod's rather violent, possibly autobiographical *Theogony*).

Thanks to the fact that Hesiod's father was poor and a loser (Hesiod's confidential, HIPPA protected appraisal, not mine), the whole family had to sail from the relatively cosmopolitan and trade loving Cyme in Asia Minor (Anatolia) to poverty stricken Askra in Boeotian Greece. There, a young and impressionable Hesiod was made to grow up in the backwoods and hills of Kentucky (as it were), while his father hardly worked and spent his days drinking bourbon neat and watching reruns of General Hospital stretched out on an old brown couch inside their half-sized double wide. This drove the poor lad to withdraw into himself until he began hearing voices—the Heliconian Muses. So even though things turned out well in the end, and he found fame as a poet and bard, he was still angry with his father.

Finally, it comes out that Hesiod has never sailed much at all. He's only gone to Chalkis in Euboea where he won first prize in a poetry competition. So what gives?

(The important point is that he found closure, as I did with Gretchen.)

The Trade and Procurement of Wine

Well, as they say, I digress. Whether Hesiod or Homeric Greeks appreciated it much, the truth is there was much trade in wine and other goods all over the Mediterranean.

If nothing else, we know this was the case thanks to all the sunken ships marine archeologists have found off the coasts of Israel, Turkey, and France—not to mention other modern coastlines. Most of these ships contain uniquely shaped wine jars that still hold ancient wine residue. What do we know about these ceramic vessels?

According to ancient pottery experts such as the afore-mentioned Virginia R. Grace, two-handled Canaanite-Phoenician jars inspired the shape of most of these wine jars resting at the bottom of the sea or discovered in landlocked archeological digs. Skinny at the bottom, these jars grow larger and taper off at the top with a narrow neck that may be short or tall.

The same Near Eastern two-handled shape inspired early Greek wine jars called amphoras or amphorae (s. amphora). The Latin term amphora (Gk. *amphiphoreus*) consists of two words that, added together, refer to the fact that the jar may be carried on both sides by its double handles.

Early on, amphoras appear in Mycenaean Linear B clay tablet records. These same jars show up in Homer's *Odyssey*, when Telemachus orders the servant Eurycleia to draw off some wine from the larger jars in his father's storage room into amphoras, so that he can take wine with him on his journey to the Peloponnese.

Many of these Greek amphoras were impressed with a manufacturer's stamp, an ancient Near Eastern practice also observed in Mesopotamia, Egypt, and in smaller kingdoms such as Judah and Ugarit. These stamps guaranteed the provenance and vintage of the product. V.R. Grace tells us, for example, that, "Thasos, whose chief product was a famous wine, kept close control of production and sale. Standard measures have been found"—measuring amphora size, whether a quarter, half, or whole amphora—"and systematic stamping of the containers began very early"—including one Thasian stamp that bears the image of Heracles the Archer. She goes on to observe that "a good part of the Thasian wine laws can still be read in Thasos, inscribed in the marble slabs."

As for the size of the jars, the average amphora held about seven gallons. Converted to modern wine bottles, this means that an amphora held roughly thirty-five 750ml bottles or about three cases of wine.

Aside from the trade indicated by these amphoras scattered around the Greek world and at the bottom of the Mediterranean, the myths of Dionysus' journey to Hellas also imply widespread exchange in wine. Recall, Dionysus travels from Arabia through Persia, Anatolia and Thrace into Greece. This means that wine was trafficked in all of these areas, an inference backed up by archaeology.

Trade from and with the island of Lesbos is also implied by Homer's mention of Pramnian wine.

As for the explicit exchange of wine in Homer, we have to go to the seventh book of the *Iliad*, where the poet details Lemnian ships arriving to trade with the Achaean army. There he sings, "Many ships carrying wine from Lemnos were anchored nearby."

These trading vessels sailed from an island in the north Aegean that sits roughly the same distance from northern Greece and western Turkey. We met it before in Chapter 1. A volcanic island sacred to the fire and craft god Hephaestus, Lemnos possessed excellent soil for vineyards.

Homer tells us that Euneos, the son of Jason and the king of Lemnos, sent the ships (s. *naus*) and wine to the Achaeans on the shore of Ilium for two reasons. One, the wine was meant as a gift for Agamemnon and his brother Menelaus. Homer reports that Euneos gave them "a thousand measures of wine." Otherwise, the Achaeans traded or bartered other goods for the divine liquid. "From these ships the Achaeans bought their wine, some with bronze, some with iron, some with hides, some with cattle, and some again with captive slaves."

In *The World of Odysseus*, Cambridge scholar and classical studies hero Moses Finley explains that in Homer's world, "cattle were money"—but not, of course, in the sense of cash (no one in Homer carries around a few cattle in his wallet). This identification of cattle and money was largely true in much of the ancient world. In ancient Rome, for instance, the Latin word for money was *pecunia*, which comes from the word for cattle, *pecus*. (On a similar etymological note, our English word *fee* comes from the Old English word for cattle, *feoh*.)

Other methods of procurement. I've already pointed out that Homeric Greeks also obtained wine and other goods by means of raiding and plundering. This was how Odysseus and his men scored the unmixed Ismarian wine from the Cicones' man Maro. We might say that given Odysseus' godfather status, it was a forced trade Maro couldn't refuse.

Aside from trading and raiding, ancient Greeks locally grew and produced most of the wine they consumed.

Meaning? They were local and organic long before these were cool.

This is true for most of the wine you have stored in your cellar on your farm outside Athens. It's all local and organic.

Speaking of, you tell your son it's about time to have a tasting beneath the shade of the old tree in front of the house. Happily, he agrees.

Deliciously Fun Activity No. 5

Learn about wine bottles and import practices or *try an unorthodox purchase of wine*

Did you know that relative to the history of wine and wine consumption, wine bottles as we know them haven't been around for very long? It's true. It used to be that most wine was shipped in those expensive oak barrels I mentioned in the last chapter and poured out from them.

Similar to the deliciously fun activity for Chapter 1, I bid you do a little sleuthing. Find out why wine is typically served in 750ml bottles. How long has this been the case? (For a concise history of the bottle, see Matt Kramer's *Making Sense of Wine*—bibliographical details may be found in WORKS THAT INSPIRED DRINKING WINE at the end).

Also, if you didn't previously look into modern import and export practices, now's the time to do so. How does your favorite wine reach you?

Now for a truly ballsy fun activity. If you have access to a cow, even if it's just your child's or you own stuffed animal (did you know that many adults, for instance, up to 35% in Great Britain, have and sleep with a so-called comfort object), haul it into your local wine market and see if they won't barter with you. If that doesn't work, try a few rectangular bars of iron, animal skins (just make sure they're not on the endangered species list), or a few captive slaves.

(Note: if the wine clerk grows upset with you, just say you're joking.)

(Disclaimer: I hereby declare the publisher and myself not liable for any trading outcomes. If anything bad happens, blame it on Cleon or Thrasymachus.)

(Requested fee: if it works, that is, the cow swap, send me a few cases since it was my idea.*)

---

* Explanation of the fee: if an average cow is around five to six hundred dollars, you should be able to get about fifty cases of decent wine; accordingly, my fee of 'a few cases' is very reasonable. BTW, I prefer red.

5

STORING, PREPARING & SERVING
LIQUID HAPPINESS

Stand up Pontonous, mix the honey-sweet wine in the wine bowl, and distribute it to everyone reclining here in the great room, so that we can make a drink offering to Zeus, who delights in thunder.

—ANTINOUS, THE *ODYSSEY*

ALTHOUGH THE SUN is high, the ancient tree shields you and your son as you relax in the front of your farmhouse with a cup of wine and relishes to hand. Your servant leaves you with a jug of Lesbian vintage and wine from your own vineyard to compare. He's given you the new ceramic cups you purchased in Mytilene.

Sitting there, you think of Herodotus. You sat with him not more than two cycles of the moon ago in this very spot. Thinking of him reminds you of a story he told you, and so you tell it to your son.

One city wished to impress the ambassadors of another city, though the citizens of the first were actually quite poor. Hard-pressed, therefore, they came up with an ingenious plan.

Each night, when the representative men of the visiting city dined at a different house, they did so on the one existing set of golden plates, bowls, and cups that the hosting city possessed. It worked. Moving from house to house, the ambassadors believed that every family was very wealthy and always ate off golden plates and the like, just as the gods in Homer do as well as the kings of the Achaeans and of Troy.

It's true. We hear of much gold and silver in Homer—particularly among the gods living on Mount Olympus, Poseidon's "glittering golden palace" beneath the sea, and in Sleep's (Hypnos) home.

The nobility among men also prize golden cups, bowls, cauldrons, and tripods. Nevertheless, as we'll see, there were simple utensils as well.

From common to not so common language, from gold and silver to simple earthenware, Homer colorfully paints a varied picture of storing, preparing, and serving wine.

Storing Wine

In the *Odyssey*, we discover that Homeric Greeks kept wine in storerooms or cellars.

When Telemachus visits Odysseus' stockroom, he finds gold and bronze bars, clothing chests, vessels of olive oil, and rows of large storage jars (s. *pithos*) of wine. Homer references similar jars when he describes the two *pithos* jars that sit on the floor in Zeus' house. As if human fortune is a kind of wine, Achilles declares that there is good fortune in one of the jars and bad fortune in the other. Whatever wine a man gets, that's what he has to put up with. And poor you if you only get the bad! As one Homeric man says to another, "Endure it, you must, you have no other choice."

Although we cannot be certain, these *pithos* jars were most likely made of clay. Phoenix speaks of such *keramos* (clay) jars in the *Iliad*.

Since *pithos* jars were large and cumbersome, Homeric and other early Greeks drew wine into amphoras for its transportation and further storage.

Preparing Wine

Now for the fun. When it was time to drink, a servant or herald drew out (*aphussô*) the wine from the *pithos* or amphora into a mixing bowl called a *kratēr*. There he would pour (*keraiô*) a strong or pure (*zôros*) wine, one that had no admixture of water.

As an example, summon to mind the strong Ismarian wine that knocked the Cyclopes Polyphemus out after a mere four rounds of wine. Homer tells us that usually the Cicones mixed twenty measures of water with one measure of this powerful wine. So when poor Poly drank those four cups, it was really like he was tossing back eighty!

Oops.

Odysseus should have first mixed water into the wine. He should have at least followed Hesiod's advice recommending a ratio of three parts water to one part wine. (But of course that would have been contrary to the plan!)

Now when pouring out the wine into the wine bowl in order to mix it with water, the apparent goal was to pour (*egchunō* or *enchunō*) the wine to the top of the bowl, that is, to brim it. "The young men brimmed the *kratēr* with wine." How one was able to add water after that, I cannot say, unless, of course, the water went in first as the philosopher Xenophanes of Colophon later advised.

Another useful tip from the *Iliad*. If you were making a mixed drink like the one Hecamede or Circe made with Pramnian wine, barley, and feta cheese, you would need to use a bronze grater. Homer explains that Hecamede "grated goat cheese with a bronze grater" (*knēstis chalkeios*) and sprinkled it over the mixture. Amazingly, Patrick McGovern reports that such graters are known from the Late Bronze Age and that "bronze graters were a standard burial item in Iron Age warrior tombs in Greece."

Serving Wine

After the servant drew out wine from the amphora and mixed it in the *kratēr*, the cupbearer or wine-pourer (*oinochoos*) would then swing into action. (And booming from the stereo system, the man with the deep voice from Kool and the Gang would sing, "It's ladies' night!"—except for it never was in this all man's world.)

Among the gods, the cupbearer was traditionally Hebe, the youthful daughter of Zeus and Hera. However, we do witness Hephaestus shuffling around the golden floors of

Olympus and pouring the nectar at the end of Book 1 of the *Iliad*. When he does so, the gods, mean drinkers that they are, laugh at him for his misshapenness. At some point, Zeus snatches up to Olympus the mortal boy Ganymede to serve as the peach-fuzz-clad cupbearer. Apparently, he wasn't satisfied with all his feminine conquests. (Doesn't Zeus know that kidnapping and pedophilia are illegal, not to mention unethical?)

Among humans, servants typically poured the wine (*oinochoeuô*). Nevertheless, at times, comrades like Achilles' dear friend Patroclus did it, as well as heralds and other "worthy" men.

The direction of the pour was usually from left to right. We learn this from Hephaestus, who pours the nectar in this way and from the suitor Antinous just before Odysseus shoots him through the throat at the end of the *Odyssey*.

Wine Cups

The wine server ladled the wine from the mixing bowl or poured it out from a wine jug into the drinking vessels. Homer mentions at least five different kinds of cups. The most popular is the *depas*, a beaker, goblet, or chalice; it shows up nearly 100 times in the *Iliad* and *Odyssey*. The least popular is the *aleison* (cup, goblet).

Some cups were better than others. Cups that were golden (*chryseos*) or silver (*argureos*) were superior to the rustic drinking cups (s. *kissubion*) that the Cyclops Polyphemus drinks from when downing the fatal Ismarian wine or the swineherd Eumaeus uses to serve Odysseus. These are comparable to the glass jam jars you might find today in Kentucky or eastern Tennessee for drinking beer. Or if you're on a road trip, in a Cracker Barrel. From what we know, Hesiod's father was fond of these.

Kylix, one of the words most frequently used for wine-cup or chalice by later authors (the other is *potērion*), is not found in Homer. It doesn't appear much earlier than the fifth century BC. What do appear are the kinds of cups the Trojan heralds use when they pour out wine into cups (*kupellon*) for the oath sworn by the Trojans and Achaeans before Paris and Menelaus' single combat.

But more! Fifteen glorious times, Homer mentions the so-called double cup (*amphikupellos*), the cup of the Homeric drinking super hero. Why? Because, as one Greek lexicon has it, the *amphikupellos* formed a cup at both the bottom and the top. Meaning? That's right, a double pour! As soon as you shot one end, you could down the other. (Hear it loudly *mon frère*, "It's ladies night!")

Okay, more likely, the *amphikupellos* was merely a two-handled cup. But even this is cool. Either you could man-

handle it with two hands at once, or you could lift it ambidextrously with the right hand at one moment and the left at another giving both arms a decent work out.

Actually, the double handled cup would be great for a lefty in this prejudiced, right hand leaning world. If you're a lefty like me, you probably know what I mean. Whenever you buy a souvenir cup from, say, Niagara Falls, Las Vegas, or the UFO museum in Roswell,

New Mexico, the picture or wording is only on one side of the cup. And yes, that's right (no pun intended), it is the side that's convenient for the right-hander to look at as he or she happily sips his morning coffee or drinks a mug of beer.

Examples of *amphikupellos* cups? Achilles uses a two-handled cup to pour wine out to his beloved friend Patroclus. The bard Demodocus drinks from one in Alcinous' house in between riffs and refrains.

Yet these doubles were nothing compared to the drinking rock star Nestor's cup (rock star in the sense of an old Mick Jagger). Let me explain.

Nestor's was a beautiful cup (*depas*) that the old man had brought from home in Pylos, one fastened with gold tacks. But here's the rock star status thing: rather than the usual super heroic double handler, this golden cup had four handles! (Do you hear the angels of heaven above singing and the demons in Tartaros below groaning with jealousy?) And above two of the handles, two doves were perched as if they were drinking from the cup. How sweet is that? Lastly, the cup was so heavy that most men could hardly lift it from the table. Not the old horseman Nestor, though. He could lift it easily with one hand. No. Big. Deal.

You laugh imagining this Cyclopean cup.

Your son laughs too before asking you what Homer's heroes would have done if they wanted to take wine on a voyage and they didn't want to haul along a heavy amphora.

You tell him that in such a case they would pour wine into goatskin sacks (*askos aigeios*). But typically they would take amphoras full of wine, just as Telemachus did when he sailed to the mainland.

Which in a very roundabout way reminds you. You must respond to Hipponicus' invitation for the wine party he's having in a few weeks. He's asked you to send some of the Lesbian wine you purchased in Mytilene along as a party favor. You've already decided to send him an amphora. Not only do you like him, but you also need him to do a favor for you that you've been considering for some time.

Meanwhile, you raise your cup and have a drink. What could be better than sitting beneath the shade of a tree and drinking a fragrant wine with your oldest son?

Deliciously Fun Activity No. 6

Experiment with preparing and serving wine

Have you ever added water to your wine? Sounds nasty, right? Well, as you now know, mixing water into wine was common in the ancient Greek world. So why not give it a try?

While you're experimenting with water and wine, try mixing it in a large bowl. Afterwards, drink your wine out of different cups and small bowls. Experiment with a variety of shapes and materials: broad and shallow, narrow and deep; ceramic, wood, metal, and glass.

I don't recommend skull cups, however. Although Herodotus reports that the barbaric Scythians used them, the Scythians weren't Greek. And so being a good, proper, and snobby Greek, you shouldn't use them either. (Unless you really want to. Then, if you wish to tip back a skull with your warrior buddies, it should be in celebration of a glorious kill. In fact, you can't drink out of the annual wine bowl unless you've killed an enemy over the course of the year. No kill, no glory—and no wine. Only shameful soup for you. Sorry.) (Also, you may wish to stretch a skin across the bowl of the skull or gild it if you're rich.) (On another note, Herodotus reports that the Scythians had weed bonfires or smoke-vapor "baths"—as in smoking *kannabis*, aka *cannabis sativa*, marijuana, the original reefer. The good historian colorfully explains that the Scythians "howl like wolves" in their "delight" while taking these "baths." I wonder if this kind of weed-product is coming to Colorado soon? But seriously, where's the sour grapes king Pentheus of Thebes when we truly need him?)

Aside from mixing and drinking trials, I would also suggest experimenting with storing your wine in different places—like a steamy hot car, for instance, or behind the dead bush out back on a sub-freezing day in January. But I don't want you to waste Dionysus' precious gift, so I won't. That would be sinful and worthy of a one-way trip to Tartaros (at least for a while—with Socrates, I don't believe in eternal damnation).

Blessings.

Amphora II

Delighting in Ancient Greek Wine

6

THE USES & ENJOYMENT OF WINE

The young men filled the wine bowls full and served them to all, first offering libations to the everlasting gods who rule over all.

—HOMER, THE *ILIAD*

SEVERAL WEEKS HAVE passed. It's a relatively cool night in Pyanepsion (what later people will call parts of October and November), and you're at a symposium hosted by your friend, the very wealthy Hipponicus, (aka Horse-Victor). He's the son of the elder Callias who fought against the Persians at the epic battle of Marathon some fifty years ago, the namesake of Hipponicus' own son, Callias.

You know how the older Callias made his money, right? No—not in the wine trade. He loaned slaves to the Athenian owned silver mines at Laurium when Athens was building up her navy under the direction of Themistocles. Hipponicus still makes a fortune that way.

When the slaves attending the door let you in, you walk through the courtyard and toward the *andrōn*, the men's room. Just before entering, you notice an attractive older girl peeping out through a window adjoined to the *gynaeceum*, the women's quarter. She must be Hipparete (Horse-Excellence), you guess, who will later marry Alcibiades.

Speaking of, the dashing young Alcibiades and the goodly Agathon call out to you as you pass through the door. Happy to see them, you're not very happy however when they greet you as "old man." But it's true. Your oldest son is closer in age to them than you are. You're better matched with Hipponicus and his cohort.

When you enter, your eyes sweep the room. Standing about and reclining on couches, you see the physician Eryximachus, Diodotus a man you much admire, and Nicias recently returned from the battle success of fortifying Minoa opposite Megara. There are also Protagoras of Abdera, the businessman Callicles, the sophist Prodicus of Ceos, and Callias, Hipponicus' son. And, gods no, you spot that beastly man Thrasymachus with the feeling you get when you suddenly notice bird droppings in your wine. *Zeus!* You'd rather see the demagogue Cleon than this man. On second thought, you'd rather they both drink hemlock in Hades so you never have to see or hear either man again!

Then, thank the gods, with considerable pleasure relative to the psychic pain you've just experienced, you realize there's another man hiding in the shadowy corner. He's facing away from you and toward the wall. You know him, though, because of his bare feet and tattered appearance, even from behind. It's Socrates, the philosopher. You smile.

No, you realize, there are two men. When at first you think Socrates is talking to himself, as people know him to do, especially when he falls into one of those fits of abstraction, you suddenly realize that a very young Timotheus of

Miletus is standing in front of him against the wall. They must be talking about music—since the latter is one of the best lyre players in Hellas right now, topping all the charts.

Aside from all the symposium-goers, there are the many servants—the meat carver, the wine steward, the food servers, the cupbearers, the perfume daubers, and others.

You walk in and mingle.

After some time, Hipponicus directs everyone to recline on a couch, and you take a meal while listening to Timotheus of Miletus play. He's plugged in to a small black amp. Although many appreciate his new style and the so-called ant-runs he performs up and down the lyre—what later music aficionados might term a hard-rocking, head-banging solo—others grumble at  the new music and the additional string he's added to the instrument. These traditionalists forget about it, though, when the party songs begin and the wine drinking commences in earnest.

But hold on. You don't just throw back the wine as one might at any other party where they toss back one cold Bud after another pulled from a 15.5 gallon keg.

No, the ancient Greeks used and enjoyed wine in many different ways. And some of these, no party could safely do without.

Happily, we can trace most of these uses back to Homer and other early Greeks. Let's see.

Refreshment and Relaxation

Homeric and other early Greeks delighted in wine for many reasons. Most obvious was the sense of reinvigoration and ease it gave to the drinker, whether at the end of a slogging long battle or the completion of many months of hard toil on the farm.

We witness the latter when Hesiod kindheartedly bids his brother Perses to relax and take some time off, a wish that he could have just as easily directed at you in the midst of the harvest.

By then, you've sweated long and hard for the past two months harvesting your crops beneath the blistering sun that withers the skin. *Dang!* It's mid-July, and the golden thistles are blossoming, cicadas are chirping, and, declares Hesiod, the "goats are fattest and richest in milk, the wine is the best, and the women are, well, that's when the women are horniest—even though the men are powerlessly all dried out!" (Note: Hesiod's meaning regarding *los hombres* is somewhat uncertain here.)

Despite this rather unmanly condition, one that may call for certain later medications with potential four-hour long side effects, Hesiod goes on with the instruction to chill out we've all been waiting for. "At that time, find a shady spot beneath a tree or rock ... [and eat] barley-cakes made from the best flour and milk, goat cheese, and roasted meat from forest fed cows."

No problem, Hes-dawg, happy to oblige. But what about an adult beverage?

We've already encountered Hesiod's response in an earlier chapter. So to repeat, here's what you do. Find "some Bibline wine" and drink it "sitting in the shade ... with your face directed toward fresh-blowing Zephyrus."

You do. And drunk, you believe you've died and gone to the Isles of the Blessed, where the sun shines at just the right temperature, the heroes live on without care, and the Earth freely gives everything a man could possibly desire.

As for the former scenario, a cup of wine for refreshment during the course of a battle or at its end, Hector's mother Hecuba indicates how this worked.

Having just returned from the battlefield, Hector encounters his mother in Priam's palace. "My child," she queries, "why have you left the spirited fight? Look what they've done to you!"

Hector's bespattered with blood, soaked with salty sweat, and his hair is a dark, tasseled mess.

No matter. Hecuba swings into Greek (well, Trojan) mom-mode. (According to the *Crete Gazette*, Greek mothers are "like a broody hen who smothers her young in wings of care, love, overprotection, and oppression.") While she dabs his brow and chin, she offers, "But stay so that I may bring you a cup of honey-sweet wine." She goes on to proclaim how the wine will benefit him tremendously. "But when a man has worked hard, wine greatly increases his might, just as you have now worked so hard to defend your clansmen."

That's right: contrary to modern knowledge about the depressive effects of alcohol, drinking wine actually makes you want to get out of bed and get the job done. Like a shot of whisky in your coffee or tea. Or, try this: if you've just finished your daily exercise regime, throw back a glass of ice-cold sangria or bourbon on the rocks instead of a cup of water or a bottle of your favorite sports drink. (What do modern neurologists or nutritionists know anyway?)

The Divine Aspect

But that's not all there was to the ancient Greek delight in wine. Ancient Greeks never enjoyed wine independent of the gods. There was always a sacred dimension to the fun. Put another way, they always imbibed wine within the confines of a religious context or with a religious mindset.

When Hecuba makes the above honey-sweet wine offer to Hector, she immediately goes on to say, "...so that you may make a drink offering to Zeus and the other immortals first, and then you will benefit from it also, if you drink."

Hecuba sets the act of drinking into the framework where it belongs, where every ancient Greek from Homeric times onwards would have put it. If you drink, you do it with and for the gods. We see this connection in Homer relative to animal sacrifice, general drinking and pouring out libations, and in the process of swearing an oath.

Wine and the Sacrifice

In Homer, the Greeks used wine to prepare or anoint the animal sacrificial victim.

Old Nestor remembers well the day he and Odysseus came to Peleus' house recruiting men for the Achaean army. Strolling into the courtyard, they saw Menoetius, Achilles, and Achilles' father. "And the old man Peleus, the driver of chariots, was burning the fat thigh-bones of a bull to Zeus who delights in thunder." In his right hand, "Peleus held a golden cup, pouring out a drink offering of sparkling wine upon the blazing sacrificial victim."

Likewise, when the priest Chryses sacrifices to appease Apollo after Agamemnon returned his daughter to him, he

baptizes the animal's flesh with wine. After praying and flinging barley grain to the wind, he and the other priests slit the throats of the victims, skin them, and carve away the meat. Finally, they pour "sparkling wine" over the burning flesh before feasting.

Wait a second, you might protest. Why are we squandering all that quality sparkling wine?

In answer to your grave question, I say that we're not wasting the wine. Rather, we always reserve a portion of Dionysus' divine liquid and a portion of the victim for the god or gods as their rightful portion. We know we ought to do this thanks to Zeus himself.

Defending Priam and Troy against "greedy Hera" (really Zeus?) who wishes to annihilate the city, her husband declares, "Never was my altar in Ilium lacking the equal feast, or the drink offering, or the smoke of fat rising from the burnt offering. For that is the portion that we gods attained by lot, our right and privilege."

You see, it's theirs. Just like shouting out "shotgun" to get the front seat next to the driver of the chariot, the gods called it and got their portion first.

On another note, sometimes a god manifests him or herself during the sacrifice, such as Athena does to Nestor at his offering for Poseidon. "She came to me at the bountiful feast in visible, bodily form!" (He's like a kid who's seen Santa Claus beneath the Christmas tree.) When she finally flies off in the form of an eagle, all the heroes are amazed!

The truth is, however, that wherever there was a sacrificial feast, the gods were there in some manner. That revealed, unless you were an Aithiopian or an early Phaeacian, the gods usually didn't visibly feast with humans face to face. Late in the *Iliad*, Hermes tells Priam that such a human-divine party is inappropriate. Now you know.

The Reason for the Pour

Whether the gods manifested and feasted with the Greeks face to face or not, the act of making a sacrifice or pouring out a libation was always a self-interested quid pro quo act, both on the part of the god and the man sacrificing.

As an example, I offer the sad case of a very forlorn Achilles desperate before Patroclus' funeral pyre. Homer testifies that, "Standing far off from the pyre, Achilles prayed to the two winds, to the north wind Boreas and the west wind Zephyrus, and promised fair sacrificial victims [to them]."

As he pours out wine from a golden cup, he implores the winds to come and kindle the pyre. It works. The messenger goddess Iris, arrayed in many-colored light, hears the prayers and gives the dispatch to the winds who are feasting at Zephyrus' house (doubtlessly starting with a cup of Achilles' red and other hors d'oeuvres, while licking their breezy chops in anticipation of the twelve noble Trojan boys Achilles has promised to burn).

Finally, message delivered, Iris takes off to feast with the Aithiopians who are sacrificing hecatombs near the great river Oceanus at the end of the world. She assures the winds who invite her to their own feast-sacrifice that she can't miss it.

In the end, Achilles gets what he wants and so too do the gusting winds. All night long Achilles pours out libations to the winds, shimmering drinks they enjoy at their own feast, and they in turn ignite the fire that incinerates Patroclus, the poor Trojan lads, and all the other animals.

Libations

Drink offerings were always part of Homeric Greek gatherings, not only in terms of making the actual sacrifice, but also during general times of drinking and feasting.

From the *Iliad* and the *Odyssey*, we get a glimpse of how the whole process worked. First, you prepared for the feast and the libation by washing your hands. Hesiod emphatically recommends the same to his slovenly brother Perses. "Don't even think about pouring out an offering of sparkling wine to Zeus and the other immortals with unwashed hands!" Yes, brother.

Next, you appropriately cleansed the major libation vessel along with any other cups you would use during the gathering. For instance, Achilles purifies his special chalice with brimstone (sulfur), an ancient kind of powdered dishwashing soap that didn't leave spots.

Third, in most cases you poured out the libation to the gods, whether to Zeus alone, to another god, or to all the gods at once. When Achilles and Diomedes relax after cutting down pitiable Dolon who had wet his tunic with fear prior to being slain, they pour "honey-sweet wine to Athena," the immortal goddess who had helped them in their mission.

A later Homeric hymn advises that one should always offer the first and last drops to Hestia, the hearth goddess, for without her fire there are no feasts. (How right you are—unless one is eating sushi, you say, or if you're a Bacchic omophagist.) However appropriate this specific dedication must have been later on, there's no certain evidence of consecrating your pour to Hestia in Homer. Still, it's good advice.

I said that "in most cases" you pour out your libation to a god, because aside from the gods, Homer gives other reasons for pouring out a libation. One is Achilles' apparent offering to his dead friend Patroclus. "And all night long, swift Achilles ... drenched the earth with wine summoning the shade of wretched Patroclus." Similarly, Odysseus sacrifices victims and pours out a libation "to all the dead," in order to call them up from the Underworld. He does so "first with milk and honey, then with sweet wine, and finally with water." Some scholars believe this ritual might be a reflection of prehistoric practice. Who knows. Remarkably, the same custom of making a drink offering to the dead survived into the later Greek and Roman world and into early Christian practice (see *The Second Church*, R. MacMullen). Perhaps we do the same today, as ancient Greeks did, when we drink to the memory of an old friend.

These libations to the gods were always the first drops of the wine. Stated differently, you never *ever* stole a drink without first pouring to the gods. As Homer has it, "No man dared drink until he made a drink offering to the mighty son of Kronos."

Where would you pour out the liquid? Homer relates that the heroes poured it out onto the ground or onto the bare earth, i.e., Mother Earth (we might say, *from* the earth *to* the earth). We see this in the previous example where everyone first pours out a libation to Zeus. "They let the wine pour from their goblets onto the ground." This makes sense given the fact that their houses probably had packed earthen floors, as we know was the case with the main hall in Odysseus' house. Later on, Greeks designed rooms with this in mind, oftentimes with sloping floors.

Swearing an Oath

Your heroic duty accomplished in making the sacrifice and pouring out a libation, you were now in the position to drink your fill. Well, unless you were Menelaus or Paris preparing to fight each other in single combat. Then there were other things involved. Like a scary oath, for instance.

By Book 3 of the *Iliad*, everyone has had it with the war. By everyone, I mean the average Joe who wants to return home to his wife and children, not the heroes (though some of them also want to leave).

Paris himself, the Trojan sod responsible for the whole war, is shrinking back from the fight, especially before Menelaus. For this, his brother Hector chastises him. Fine, Paris responds with a huff. I'm not afraid of him. I'll take him on in single combat. The deal: whoever wins will get to keep Helen and all her wealth. (*Lucky Helen.*)

When Menelaus eagerly agrees to this arrangement, the two sides come together to swear an oath in the neutral zone between the Achaean and Trojan army. There, two wooly lambs accompany a priest who piously glides to the middle holding a goat wineskin full of ruddy wine. Others carry forward a radiant wine bowl and golden cups.

After washing their hands and mixing the wine, Agamemnon takes his sharp knife and cuts tufts of knitted hair from the lambs' heads. When the heralds distribute it, Agamemnon makes a prayer with his hands lifted high in the ancient *orans* posture (imagine your arms raised up like the letter Y). If Paris wins, he shouts out, he'll get Helen and her things; if Menelaus wins, he will. He finishes by appealing to the gods. May father Zeus, who loves thunder, and Helios, who sees and hears all, and the rivers and those in the world below take vengeance if either of these men swears a false oath! All around the men cry out, Amen! And so it will happen.

Agamemnon now cuts the lambs' throats with "the ruthless bronze," and like wine, their blood flows out onto the ground.

Finally, other chief men draw wine from the mixing bowl into the golden cups and pour it out. As they do so, they pray to the everlasting gods invoking a kind of sympathetic magic, where the initial act influences or causes another thing to be or happen (similar to the way voodoo dolls work—you poke it with a pin thereby stabbing and hurting the person it represents). "Glorious Zeus and you other immortal gods, whichever army of the two first breaks their oaths, may their brains be poured out onto the ground just as this wine is—their brains and their children's; and may their wives be conquered."

Funny thing; that's exactly what happens after the Trojans break the oath. There must be something to this whole sympathetic magic thing. I may have to go to the voodoo house in New Orleans to check it out.

In any event, I don't know about you, but the ancient Greek use and enjoyment of wine makes our own modern drinking seem somewhat dull. All we do is uncork, pour, and drink. And repeat.

Nothing in the modern world really approaches the excitement and meaning of ancient drinking practices except perhaps the wine use of practicing Jews during Shabbat (the Sabbath) and Pesach (Passover), or those rituals still performed in the Roman Catholic and Orthodox Christian churches that offer up bread and wine to the god (*ho theos*) (now capitalized as the one and only God). According to the Roman liturgy, the wine is "poured out" for the many (Latin *pro multis*). But of course here, in comparison with your average Greek pouring, everything is reversed. Rather than the ancient quid pro quo swap (I'll pour out this wine if you give me that), the blood of the God (Jesus the Christ) is freely poured out by the God for the good of the many so that the many might become God by drinking-participating in the wine-blood (and bread-body) of the God.

Fascinatingly, many scholars believe that the Christian rite was influenced by the Eleusinian Mysteries. During the rite of this ancient mystery religion that men and women practiced for two thousand years, one mystically joined with the sacrificial victim Zagreus-Dionysus (sacrificed by the Titans), was purified of sin, and was finally given a happy afterlife, not to mention various boons in the present life. Like the Christian ritual, it was a good deal (in addition to all the drinking involved).

Song and Games

Well, let's return to the party. It's time to sing and play some drinking games. But first, the set up and the flow.

The sixth-century poet and early philosopher Xenophanes of Colophon—the man who famously hypothesized that if horses or cattle could paint and make sculptures, then they would make the gods look like horses and cattle—tells us how a symposium should go in a poem he wrote. Here's the kernel of what he suggests: starting off, we should make sure the floor, our hands, and all the cups are clean (sound familiar?). Then, as we recline on couches placed around the *andrōn*, the servants garland us and offer sweet-scented perfume in a shallow dish. To the side, the mixing-bowl (*kratēr*) is brimming, with additional amphoras or other jars full of mellow wine in the storeroom. In the center of the room, the altar bursts with colorful flowers, and fragrant smoke drifts upwards from the slowly burning frankincense. Golden-brown bread, goat cheese, and thick honey are available for snacking. Soon the servants will serve the main course. Yet first, cautions Xenophanes, it's good to pour out a libation and hymn the god. Of course! Who would forget that? So, perhaps a hymn to Apollo, Pan, or Zeus. Then we can drink, but only so much as we can walk home by ourselves without an attendant (says our man Xenophanes). Wagging his finger, he finishes: if one needs a designated walker, then one has had too much. Period.

After obliging the gods and drinking a first cup, we can now turn to singing party songs accompanied by the lyre. (Long parenthetical remark: I'm reminded of my own childhood, when I used to sleep out in the backyard in a tent with my best friend Billy.  Among the many things we liked to do—such as drawing up lists of the girls we fancied or making unspeakable bodily noises whose results would have been masked by the frankincense smoke had we been at a symposium—we would sing songs like, "Splish, Splash, I Was Takin' a Bath," "On Top of Spaghetti," and "The Battle Hymn of the Republic" from his Cub Scout sing-along book. Coincidentally, I had my first wine with Billy in fourth grade—as I remember it, we stole some of my dad's horrendous jug wine and gulped it down out of a yellow plastic breakfast juice cup. It's no wonder why I didn't care for wine for a long while thereafter.)

Anyway, we may sing some of the ancient Greek songs in honor of a god, say Athena, Demeter, Artemis, Pan, or even Fate herself if we're hard up for a good future. Other songs might praise a man for his victory in the games or past men for their heroic deeds in a particular battle. Take Demodocus who sings of "the glorious deeds of men" in the *Odyssey*. One of his songs is about "the quarrel of Odysseus and Achilles." Sweet, love that one. Speaking of, Achilles similarly sings of "the outstanding feats of men" when the ambassadors come to his shelter in the ninth book of the *Iliad*. He does so while playing a beautifully decked out lyre for Patroclus (did you know that, aside from being a tornadic fighter, Achilles was also a glam rock star?). Other songs list the best things a man could possibly desire— justice, health, and to get what you really want. As one version has it, "To be healthy is best for a mortal man, second is to be handsome in body, third is to be wealthy without trickery, and last is to be young with your friends."

Great, you think. You guess the last on the list is out of your hands. Remember? Agathon and Alcibiades earlier labeled you, "Old man" when you entered the *andrōn*. Oh well. You drink another cup. (As for me, I think of being young with Billy and the list of girls we thought pretty: Gina, Laurie, Mindy, and others. When Mindy moved away from Fort Worth to Kansas, we made a light blue t-shirt with dark blue lettering that read, "I'm a Mindy Lover.")

Some songs were serious and some were playful, even bawdy. Speaking of, as the drinking grows truly serious, someone nearly always recommends a game of kottabos.

For those of you who aren't familiar with the game, this is when you take turns flinging drops of wine and the drudge at the bottom of the cup at a target some feet distant. The one who best hits the target wins.

But that's not all! Just as you make your fling, you make a wish for amorous success with someone you've had your eye on. It may be a woman you know (but careful—this is very dangerous, especially if she's married!). Or, in imitation of Zeus whose sense of ethics is questionable, it may be a peach-fuzz sporting young lad you've had your eye on. As the fifth-century poet Theognis of Megara has it in one of his drinking songs, "Happy the man who goes home and engages in amorous exercise, sleeping with a handsome boy all day long." I always picture (a legal and ethical version of) this song performed to the hard rocking tune of AC/DC's "You Shook Me All Night Long"—you know, the earth quaking, the walls shaking, the mythological lovemaking. I can only imagine Timotheus of Miletus doing an ant-run on his lyre alongside Angus Young on lead guitar. (That would be inconceivably honey-sweet!)

Well, if you didn't win at kottabos, and you still had a hankering for a little playful activity, there were oftentimes *hetaera* at drinking parties, companion-women for *ahem* party favors. Of course, this wasn't always the case. Nevertheless, if the legendary party animal Anacreon, who "poured out his life like a libation to Eros, the Muses, and Dionysus" is right in claiming that love is like wine, an intoxicant, then we may turn it around somewhat and say that intoxicating wine is an aphrodisiac leading one to love. Did that make sense?

Now that we're all a little tipsy, if not drunk, it's important to be fully transparent (according to the ancients, wine helps with this by loosening a man's tongue and providing a window onto his soul) and admit that not all partygoers drank. Athenaeus of Naucratis in Egypt, who

wrote the multi-volume *Philosophers at Dinner*, reports that the Athenian comic poet Phrynichus lamented that Lamprus the musician was a wimpy "water-drinker" (*hydatopotēs*). He goes on to slam him by calling him a "sniveling super-sophist" (*hypersophistēs*). What?! Say that ten times in a row after a bottle of red. In any event, you may not want to lob those words casually at a dinner party. *Just saying*.

According to Herodotus, the ancient Cappadocians living in central Anatolia were also water-drinkers. The historian explains that this is because they pursued a simple life. Apparently, they always took Dionysus to Psyra. Yet what's so simple about not drinking wine?

Okay, for certain individuals, wine doubtlessly has its ill effects. You witness them now as you spot Alcibiades making a fool of himself with Socrates. He's slobbering all over the older man.

Alcibiades is lucky, though. The philosopher would never take advantage of him. Not like *that*. Nor, quite honestly, at any time. (You want proof? See Plato's *Symposium*.)

But for the rest of us, you consider, wine has many good effects. Right? At least Homer and other early Greeks thought so.

Deliciously Fun Activity No. 7

Play kottabos like a wild man or woman in love

You may have long ago given up drinking games. If you're lucky, though, they're still part of your life. (Maybe?) Either way, why not try your hand at flinging the sediment (technically the wine lees) in your *kylix* at a target.

You don't have a *kylix*? A shallow bowl will do. Or any other cup.

You don't have any sediment because the (bloody) vintner filtered it all out? Make some. Toss some tiny breadcrumbs in and let them sink to the bottom and soak. After five minutes or so, you'll be ready to play.

Now the original game of kottabos is somewhat incomprehensible. Especially after a few unmixed cups. Accordingly, I suggest setting up a simple target that will fall over with any amount of concentrated sedimental force. Hades, if you want, just sharpie pen a simple circular target with scoring points on a sheet of white paper and hang it up with a thumbtack a few yards distant. Think of it, the whole fun anyways will be in throwing the wine drudge.

Still, if you're a stickler and insist upon playing by the rules (which you won't be by this point in the party, unless you're a water drinking, sniveling super-sophist), you may go online and check out the detailed article on kottabos in *Smith's Dictionary of Greek and Roman Antiquities*, pgs. 366-367 (available at *The Ancient Library* and other websites; by the way, *SDGRA* makes for wonderful bedtime reading if you can't get to sleep). Since you're online, you may also want to view several YouTube videos of Italians (and others) actually playing kottabos like a bunch of crazy ancient Greeks and Etruscans.

While you're playing, you may consider drinking an Italian wine called Kottabos Rosso, a Merlot and Sangiovese (the so-called 'blood of Jove' or Zeus) blend.

Whatever you do, have fun, happy tossing, and don't forget to make a wish for amorous success!

7

THE POSITIVE EFFECTS
OF DRINKING WINE

The effect of Dionysus is now dear to me, as well as Aphrodite's urgings and the Muses' inspiration—they all bring good cheer to men.
—SOLON OF ATHENS

YOU NOTICE SOCRATES breaking away from Alcibiades and strolling casually toward the wooden table laden with bread, cheese, and golden honey in a terracotta bowl. Behind him, a rather forlorn Alcibiades begins a drunken song in praise of Dionysus, "the bringer of joy," he sings, "and the eraser of pain and sorrow."

Gnawing off a piece of bread, Socrates pivots toward Alcibiades, and grinning widely with that twinkle he gets just before he's going to demonstrate his love for a friend who is really unlovable, he calls out, "I agree with you, dear man. The god is worthy of our praise. But I wonder why?"

By now, the *andrōn* has grown quiet in response to Alcibiades' sloppy singing and Socrates' probing question. So much so, that glancing around, the philosopher makes a proposal.

He starts by quoting the poet Theognis of Megara. "Wine: I praise you for some things and censure you for others; I am unable to fully love you or hate you. You're good and noble, and also the opposite."

Alcibiades, who's truly very clever despite his sloppiness, finishes the poem for Socrates. Yes, he sings, "But what wise man would dare attempt to praise or blame wine?"

"Ah!" counters Socrates. "But that's exactly what I propose. Don't you believe what Herodotus reports about the Egyptian king Amasis?"

"I thought you didn't care for Herodotus."

"Whether I like him or not has nothing to do with it. Besides, it's what the man says about the gods I don't like. But never mind. I like what he says about wine … at least what he has Amasis declare."

"Remind me."

"I will. When certain of his officials were upset with him for drinking and joking at the end of a hard day's work, Amasis argued that there is a time for serious work and a time for fun. Man is like a bow and its string, he reasoned. If the bow is always strung and taut, then it will be useless in time of need. Consequently, one must loosen and unstring the bow occasionally. In like manner, a man should be serious at times—tautly strung—and at others frivolously fun—loose and unstrung.

"I take from this that wine is both good and bad. It's good at the right moment, the time to relax, and bad when a man should be serious and working.

"In any case, here's what I propose, gentlemen. Let's have a discussion. Let's first give speeches in praise of wine. Afterwards, we'll blame it for all the evil wine brings to mortal men. Lastly, if you're up to it, we'll figure out how to best deal with its negative effects. What do you say?"

"A fine idea," Agathon responds, chuckling, "I for one have plenty to say in praise of wine."

With this boastful claim that he made more in jest than earnestly, everyone agrees that Agathon should begin the festival in praise of Dionysus.

Straightening himself on the couch, therefore, he does, now taking himself quite seriously.

Wine Satisfies

Agathon: "I assume you all are familiar with how often Homer references wine. I recall that Niceratus, the son of Nicias, once tried to count all the times the poet mentions wine of any kind or getting drunk in the *Iliad* and the *Odyssey*. I don't remember the exact number he came up with, but it was hundreds of times.

Have you ever considered why Homer mentions wine so often? I, for one, have. I believe it's because we never tire of hearing about it. The reference to wine increases our thirst, the desire in our spirits and hearts for Dionysus' ecstatic release. Strangely, we enjoy experiencing the tension of this augmented desire. We do because the longing for wine is the doorway to finding satisfaction and feeling good. Who doesn't want to feel good?"

"I do!" cries out Alcibiades, and everyone laughs.

(It's a brilliant point. The crazy thing is that modern neuroscience would side with the essentials of Agathon's argument. What happens is that when Homer mentions wine, and we consequently think about getting up from the couch and uncorking a bottle, a small burst of dopamine explodes along the circuits of our brain and we feel good. It's the joy of anticipation. As Loretta Graziano Breuning writes in *I, mammal: why your brain links status and happiness*, "Dopamine signals the expectation of reward"—rather than the attainment of the reward, as was the old view. It's probably why I feel like drinking wine whenever I sit down to type this book. Anyway, back to Agathon.)

By now, he's quoting Solon, the Athenian statesman who did so much to reform Athenian politics nearly two hundred years before. "'The effect of Dionysus is now dear to me, as well as Aphrodite's urgings and the Muses' inspiration. They all bring good cheer to men.'

"That sums it up, friends. Wine satisfies desire. I recall the passage in Homer where Nausicaa's mother Arete packs snacks in a basket—meat, bread, and relishes—and fills a

goatskin with wine. Why does she do this? She does so because the snacks and wine will satisfy her daughter's and maiden friend's desires when they're out washing laundry by the stream. It's what any good mother would do! That's what wine is all about. It pleases us. Wine is something you drink when thirst bids you to imbibe.

"But how does it satisfy? Doubtlessly Arete thought it would strengthen and revivify her daughter after working hard all morning. Circe makes a similar point to Odysseus. When he's sitting around all worn out and disheartened, she gives him wine to restore his spirit (*thumos*). Wine makes a man feel reinvigorated, full of spirit and courage.

"Most importantly, wine is sweet to the taste and enjoyable. In wine, therefore, we find a great deal of pleasure and happiness. Recall Stesichorus of Sicily's command: 'Dear friend, drink and gladden your heart with the abundant feast!'"

Just then, Alcibiades stands up, lifts his cup, and sings out, "I raise my cup to Dionysus who grants oblivion when love is denied! In honor of Anacreon, I pronounce, 'I have become a drinker!'"

Everyone laughs again, especially Socrates. Thrasymachus (*grrr*), however, soon grows impatient with Alcibiades' attempt to take over. Knowing the sophist all too well, you know he wants to make the same move, but he doesn't want to be seen for committing such a breach of custom. Finally, he adroitly silences Alcibiades by promising him the next turn to talk.

When Agathon carries on again, he explains how wine gladdens the heart. "Dionysus is the delight of man, making him cheerful. So with Theognis of Megara, I declare that I'm happy drinking well! Let's take his advice, then, gentlemen, let's take pleasure in drinking, and let the gods worry about what will happen afterwards."

Cheering erupts in the *andrōn*. Everyone applauds Agathon and agrees to his very sober suggestion. No more worries!

Then Alcibiades rises once again to begin his own panegyric to wine. As he does, you eye Socrates who smiles. Alcibiades is as hammered as can be.

Wine Relieves Pain and Tranquilizes

Alcibiades storms over to Socrates, and after placing a hand on his shoulder, he turns to you and the others and pleads, "But what happens when things don't work out? What if you experience a reversal or worse yet a defeat? Then, I say, then wine is revealed for its best effects! It's then I praise the god!"

His shoulders broaden as he gulps down another cup. Citing Anacreon, or the men who composed in his style, he cries out, "'The wine god—he grants the suffering man endurance, and the young man fearlessness in love!'

"So along with Simonides of Ceos, I command, 'Drink! For wine is man's defense against unhappiness, the repeller of all anxieties.'"

He stumbles. "Gods I'm drunk—but I feel brilliant! So again, I quote, 'Let us drink! I praise the son of Semele and Zeus who granted men wine to make them forget their sorrows!'"

You can't place the quote, so you ask Alcibiades who it is. When he tells you, you can't help but think of your recent voyage to Alcaeus of Mytilene's island and hometown. A chill runs down your neck and back thinking of the chore your fellow citizens sent you and the other men to accomplish. You curse the god of war recalling that Athena herself called Ares the bane of men.

As you briefly remember your weeks there and the amphoras of wine and drinking set you brought home, Alcibiades promises and delivers a few other choice morsels of advice from Alcaeus. When a friend dies, for example, he counsels a good drunk. "Now we must drink with all our strength and get drunk, since Myrsilus is dead." So too when a battle is around the bend and your heart is enraged with anger and hatred for the enemy. "Let's forget anger with drink until the war god demands we take up arms." In general, wine is a cure-all for every grief. "We must not surrender our hearts to the distress we feel, Bycchis; no, loathing matters will not help. The best medicine is scoring some wine and getting drunk."* Wine even helps when Zeus is angry with Hera and thunders all day long. Then, assures Alcaeus, wine will help you to defeat the weather. "Light a fire, freely mix the honey-sweetened wine, and put a nice pillow beneath your head."

After this, Alcibiades suddenly shifts topic, tone, and mood. "But what about *my* future?" he asks, his shoulders slumping. "Will I ever amount to anything? Will I obtain the glory I deserve? And will I find love?

"How right Anacreon was to ask and declare, 'How can we know what is destined? Man's life is unclear, uncertain. So then? As for me, I wish to be drunk and dance, to anoint myself with sweet-smelling perfume and play.'"

Happier now, if only a bit, as if a melancholy happiness, the delightful man goes on, "'Whenever I drink wine, all my anxious thoughts go to sleep. But what do I care about all

---

* The line reminds me of a saying that was popular in Evelyn Waugh's family (the English author of *Brideshead Revisited*, *The Loved One*, and other wonderful novels). When facing something trying and adverse, you resolutely said, "I do not repine" or "I shall not repine." Instead of a good repine, you would drink choice wine (Waugh was often pickled). Apparently the saying hailed from Psmith, a P.G. Wodehouse character. See Alexander Waugh's, *Fathers and Sons: The Autobiography of a Family*.

these troubling thoughts anyway? I too must die, even if I do not wish to—so why should I allow my thoughts to wander grievously about life and living? Let's drink the wine of fair Dionysus, the Loosener! For when we drink, our concerns go to sleep.'"

With that, Alcibiades sinks down into his soft couch and a servant fills his cup twice over as he tosses off one drink before asking for another.

You suppose anxiety is now the least of his concerns. His mind seems a blank, and soon he demonstrates the last positive effect of wine he praised when he quietly drifts off to sleep. The scene reminds you of the time Athena shed oblivion on the suitors when they were deep in their cups in Odysseus' great house.

Bonne nuit, mon ami, you whisper (well, if you knew French; if not, Good night, my friend).

Wine Brings People Together

Protagoras of Abdera speaks up next. Clearing his throat before commencing, he dryly observes, "I believe Alcibiades has just demonstrated the opposite of what I would like to praise Dionysus for.

"In short, wine brings men together and, if they can stay awake long enough and drink with measure,"—he pauses as everyone laughs—"it serves as a social bond. And for that, wine is worthy of our admiration. It's the glue (*kolla*) of the polis. Since Alcibiades likes Alcaeus of Mytilene so much, with him I say, 'Drink and get drunk with me, O Melanippus!' It's the *with me* part that's important, friends, not the getting drunk!

"I believe Odysseus spoke well when he proclaimed to the Phaeacians that 'there is nothing better or more delightful than when a whole people make merry together, with the guests sitting orderly to listen, while the table is loaded with bread and meats, and the cup-bearer draws wine and fills it for every man.'

"One might even say that the family, household, or people that drinks together stays together. This is why the Spartan equals, the *homoioi*, form into drinking and eating clubs, the *syssitia*. These clubs strengthen their tie to one another. The rest of us Greeks do the same, but to a much lesser extent. Of course, this is what the symposium is all about, right?

"On a similar note, Homer tells us about Eetion's son Podes, who was a dear drinking friend to many Trojans. Unlucky for him, red-haired Menelaus dropped him with a spear through his gut and he fell to the ground with a thud.

"And don't forget the *scolia*, the drinking song, that goes, 'Drink with me, sport with me, and join me in wearing a crown of garlands—be enraged with me when I am mad and sober when I'm not drinking.'

"Indeed, this brings me to my final point. When drink with others, we ought to conform to what others, in general, are doing. I don't mean to suggest there is any absolute right or wrong. Rather, as you well know, man is the measure of all things, whether good or bad. So as Theognis of Megara advises, we should stay sober if others aren't drinking and get drunk when others are. 'It's shameful to be drunk in sober company and sober when others are drunk.' So let's drink men—together!"

Wine Strengthens and Grants Courage and Happiness

Your host Hipponicus sits forward at this point and proposes to praise wine in terms of the power and fortitude it gives a man. Being Spartan-like and so a man of few words unless necessity demands more, he explains that he'll be brief.

"It was the great epinician poet Pindar who stated what we all know and have experienced, that a man's voice grows confident when he stands next to the mixing bowl, drawing off cup after cup of wine. This is true no matter the activity.

"As Hecuba tells Hector, wine 'increases a man's spirit and mighty force.' Elsewhere Homer asserts that wine and meat are a man's *menos kai alkes*, his strength, prowess, and courage. He further claims that full of wine and other victuals, "a man is able to fight all day long, carrying on with the grim work of war until the battle's end." (Which leads

 me to shrug and observe: although I can imagine driving a tank into battle, I can't imagine going into battle tanked.)

Nevertheless, despite my own imagination handicap, Hipponicus goes on: "What a boon this is—wine! Think of it this way, friends. If wine lends us courage in ample measure, then if we recall the inspirational words that Pericles so recently

spoke to us in the first year of the war, we can confidently praise wine as the root of happiness. Let me explain.

"Speaking of the heroes who had died for our sake, Pericles advised us to take them as our model and thus never decline the dangers of war. Why? Because—and here's the crucial part—happiness is the fruit of freedom, and freedom is the fruit of courage in warfare.

"I'll end with this. If we drink, we know from Homer that we'll be strong and courageous; if we're courageous, we'll dare to fight; and if we dare to fight, we'll be free; and free, we'll be happy—for free men are happy men."

Eryximachus, the physician, smiles and admits, "I've never quite thought of it that way." Then he starts, "But—"

"What now?" sighs Hipponicus. "Have I misspoken? Have I left something out?"

"Not at all," Eryximachus assures him. "You're speech was quite to the point. Exemplary. Lapidary."

"But?"

"I cannot truly blame you, but you left out that one blessing without which there can be no true happiness."

"Please, then, heir of Asclepius, speak you mind."

Wine Gives Health

Eryximachus does. "Since you left it out, and since it is so important, I must quote Ariphron of Sicyon at length:

> Health, eldest and most august among the blessed gods among mortals, may I abide with you until my life is over, and may you willingly remain with me: for any joy in wealth, or in children, or in a king's godlike rule over men, or in

Aphrodite's desires, or in any other pleasure or rest from toils that has been brought to light by the gods to men, is empty without you. With you, blessed Health, life flourishes and joy shines in the intimate discourse of the Graces; but without you, no man is happy.

"Fortunately, we may turn to wine as a source of health. Therefore, wine is both the font of health and happiness. Not only does the wine god help us endure and love, but Anacreon informs us that when men gather in the grapes, make, and consume wine, then they stay healthy in body and mind throughout the year.

"Now, the question is how does wine help. For the answer to this query, I turn to my own mentor Hippocrates. Although he has not yet flourished as we customarily say, he's already composed a treatise stating what kinds of food to eat during the different seasons, and how much water we should mix into our wine."

You smile to yourself because you anticipate you've already heard part of Hippocrates' advice from your wife (who watches the ancient Greek equivalent of Oprah and Dr. Phil; not you; you only watch HSN, the Heroic Sports Network, which now has mock battles replete with phalanx scrums on every day but for Tuesday, Wednesday, and Friday—unless you're a college mock battle fan, then you can catch a game on Friday as well [thank the gods!]; chariot racing, i.e. HASCaR, the Hellenic Association of Swift Chariot Racers, takes place during  the usual slot on Saturdays and Sundays). Anyway, enough of the manly man stuff; back to Eryximachus who is discussing what to eat, when, and how to mix the wine.

"During the winter we should eat dry bread, roasted meats, and undiluted wine. The goal is to keep the body warm and dry. At the year's opposite pole, during the summer, we want to keep the body cool and soft or wet, so we should eat boiled meat and vegetables and soft cereals cooked in water. As for the wine, we should then add a good measure of water. Between these two, when winter morphs into summer during spring and the other way around during fall, we should gradually add or take away water from our wine. The two are transition seasons.

"According to Hippocrates,"—whose very name, Horse-Power, distractedly reminds you of HASCaR and the big race that's coming up in a few days and the four big guns behind the chariot you hope will win—"we have to be very careful with the way we drink. If not, there may be bad consequences in terms of health and otherwise.

"And that, dear men, is all I have to say."

With one more reminder about the importance of health, Eryximachus finishes his speech, which everyone judges quite appropriate for a man of his profession.

Then Socrates stands. "Bravo!" he shouts out, applauding. "You've all lived up to the task. So far, at least. Now, unless anyone has anything more to say in praise of wine's positive effects, let's turn to the negative."

You all agree, and after the servants pour out another round, young Callias volunteers to begin the blame game in the manner of an Iambic poet.

Deliciously Fun Activity No. 8

Track the positive effects of drinking in your own life

You may be thinking, what's so fun about this activity, tracking drinking's positive effects? *Buena pregunta, amigo.*

My response is the same point I made relative to the simple premise of this whole book. The more you know about drinking, including your own drinking, the more enjoyable it will be for you.

Yeah sure, you know imbibing wine is good, but why? Think about it. How is it good? When? With whom?

If nothing else, take a gander at why you sense wine the way you do and why it is pleasurable, from the moment its sweet fragrance wafts up to your nose, to when it first hits your tongue, to when the alcohol—the blessed C_2H_5OH—rafts around your blood stream and ends up in the great ocean that is your brain.

Doesn't that sound fun? A little? (I think so.)

8

THE NEGATIVE EFFECTS
OF DRINKING WINE

My head is heavy with wine, Onomacritus; it overpowers me so that I am no longer the good steward of my own judgment and thoughts. And now the room in this house spins around and around! But come, let me try and stand to see if the wine holds captive my feet as well as the mind within my chest.
—THEOGNIS OF MEGARA

BEFORE CALLIAS HAS a chance to speak, Alcibiades sits straight up and shouts out, as if having a nightmare, "If you drink wine in the wrong manner, the Erinyes and the other daimons will come after you! So make another libation, dear ones, and drink another cup! And if you've sworn an oath, be sure to keep it unless you desire your brains to be poured out and splattered all over the floor!"

Everyone chuckles but for our frowning host Hipponicus. Mildly angry that young Alcibiades is making such a fool of himself and a mess of the evening, and piously worried about the gods, he suggests that Alcibiades should leave with the help of his slave. He finishes by sarcastically asserting that there's no way he'll be walking home under his own power tonight. Though, he says, he'd like to see him try.

"Rather," Alcibiades slurs, now apparently mostly awake, "I'll take a shining chariot and thunder across Athens just like Telemachus and Pisistratus stormed across the wide Peloponnese to Sparta."

Hipponicus, unable to resist smiling now, returns, "That may not be a good idea—especially in your condition."

"No, perhaps your right. But on second thought, I'd only be imitating our two ancient friends who were driving drunk when they sped from Nestor's house in Pylos to Menelaus and Helen's in … where was it?"

"You fool! You just named their destination a moment ago," Callias intervenes, hooting. "Sparta. Anyway, drunk driving or riding is never a good idea. The horses flying in the open country, the yokes and your knees shaking. Zeus, you'll just as likely fly to the ground and scrape off your skin like Eumelus did at Achilles' funeral games for Patroclus as you'll make it home. No, that's what slaves are for, right? Do you really believe Telemachus or Pisistratus was driving? Even though Homer fails to mention the driver, surely they had some thrall holding the reigns for them. Still…"

Turning to his father, Callias suggests that Alcibiades is in no condition to go anywhere. When he advises they leave him alone to sleep off his drink, everyone including Hipponicus agrees. You judge that Zeus Xenios, the guardian of guest-friends, will be pleased with the collective decision.

Then Callias begins his own speech delineating the negatives of drinking wine.

Raiding and Warfare

Callias: "I'm sure you're all familiar with the famous line in Homer that sounds the end of a feast and denotes the satisfaction of hunger for bread and thirst for wine, and the commencement of other activities. 'When the heroes put from them the desire [*eros*] for food and drink,' sings Homer, they afterwards go on to other entertainments or to sleep—like the state our good friend Alcibiades has achieved once again.

"But do you recall the great price at which this satisfaction comes? According to Odysseus, it's because of hunger and thirst that men rig their ships and raid other men.

"Now, you may think this preposterous. Clearly, we go to war for much weightier reasons than the mere need to satisfy our bellies and throats!

"I think not. Indeed, I agree with Odysseus. Such war is necessary. Think of it: our world doesn't provide enough for everyone. As Hesiod understands and states the problem, Zeus has hidden the means of surviving and living, and so much toil is required to procure them—hard work on a farm or the grim work of war on the battlefield. Either way, when it comes to good food and wine, only the few like us can enjoy what we want, whereas the many have to go without, barely surviving. This is only right. The strong dominate the weak and take what they can. The gods demonstrate this truth just as men always have.

"Even so, I must admit that human existence would be better if every man and woman could have an easy life, a divine life where bread is ample and the wine flows. As it stands, though, Odysseus is right.

"Consequently, when the belly or throat urges us on as a master compels a slave, we do what it takes to survive and procure bread and wine. To quote the hero, 'Constantly does my belly bid me eat and drink, and makes me forget everything else, commanding that it be satisfied.' For many, as for the beggar Odysseus in the *Odyssey*, the belly's insistence leads to shameful and doglike behavior like begging, or to impossible feats such as fighting against the younger beggar Iros.

"But worst of all, as I've already noted, hunger and thirst lead men to attack one another. As Odysseus declares, 'A ravening belly may no man hide. It's an accursed plague that brings many evils upon men. Because of it, too, are benched ships made ready that bring hostile men over the unresting sea to raid, plunder, and enslave.'

"Now doubtlessly, Hesiod, if he were here, would counter that all we need to do is to work hard, and over time, we would steadily provide enough food and wine. Contrary to the way his piratical brother Perses wished to behave—just like the ship-rigging raiders Odysseus references—Hesiod's straightforward solution is the one Zeus gave us at the beginning of the Iron Age. Sweat. Toil. Hard work.

"As it stands, however, we men behave differently. So it is that thirst and hunger, wine and bread, are the bane of men. As for me, I consider this the most negative effect of wine. But who can help it?"

For a long moment, everyone is quiet, considering the brilliant argument Callias has made and the question at end.

Finally, his proud father Hipponicus suggests that the major point dovetails well with what the general Thucydides once told him about the early history of Hellas over cups of wine. He said that early on pirates had raided the coast causing farmers to be perpetually on the move. The richest soil providing the best food and wine was especially prone to attack and the change of hands. Eventually the powerful and wealthy held on to the land and grew even wealthier and more powerful. They dominated the weak. Walled cities sprung up to defend against marauders. Finally, Minos, the king of Crete, built a large navy to control the pirates at sea. As time went by, dominant men took the helm of the ship of each polis and ruled it as a tyrant. All because of fertile land, food and wine! It's only been in the last hundred years that tyranny has fallen to the rule of the people, or at least the rule of the right people.

Hearing this, your dear friend Thrasymachus cannot contain himself, so he abruptly interrupts his host in order to defend the rule of tyrants.

But thank the gods, who rule with might, Nicias intervenes. "I'll speak next," he says. To your relief, everyone heartily applauds the offer.

Roiled Thinking and Razed Judgment

Nicias: "There's little doubt that wine attacks and sacks the mind in its fortress, leaving judgment demolished, like the well-built walls of a city, and thinking, the thoughts that people the mind, confused and listlessly roaming about. As

Alcaeus of Mytilene indicated, 'Wine fetters the wits,' just as the Achaeans chained and enslaved the Trojan women and children after the fall of Troy.

"The inebriated man is therefore no longer in control of his mind, let alone his legs, body, or his tongue as Euenus of Paros has it. Telemachus makes the same point. The drunken man can't even stand straight and walk home by himself. Rather, he forcibly surrenders himself to the enemy. Indeed, if we give our attention to Anacreon, he rightly ties drinking excessive amounts of wine to insanity, giving reference to Heracles and Ajax going mad, among others.

"Who was it who said, 'People who drink strong wine possess little prudence'?"

Socrates: "It was Hipponax of Ephesus."

Nicias: "He's right, you know. Homer tells us that wine can capture your mind in such a way that it leaves you fearless—but in a bad way. You're rash; you're a fool.

"At other times, growing heavy with wine can make you pointlessly sad so that you cry and cry to no discernable end. The remarkable thing is that wine reduces the normally wise and the normally witless man to the same empty-headed condition. In that way, wine is the great equalizer."

Hipponicus: "And the gods only know how much wine has fuelled the mob toward more and more power!"

Nicias: "Well, yes. Rather than knowing their place in the city or the household, wine motivates the cowardly and slavish man to usurp the position of the fine and good man, the *kalokagathos*. But this only follows from the nature of drinking. When in his cups, a man has crazy desires. He wants to rule the whole world, have a gold and ivory house that gleams in the sun, and wheat-bearing ships carrying great stores of wealth from Egypt. Such are the thoughts of a drinker's mind and heart.

"Isn't this the acknowledged effect of wine? Think of the Thyades who revel and go wild, going out of their minds with Dionysus in the woods. How is this foolishness different from what happened to Odysseus' men when they couldn't pull themselves away from the lotus of the famous Lotus Eaters? The lotus made them forget their homes, the very thing that up to then they had lived and died for. Or again, think of when Circe served the mixture of wine, barley meal, cheese, and that unknown drug to his men some days later. As with the lotus, the wine-potion caused them to forget home and turn into pigs."

Prodicus, laughing: "Is that what wine does to us? It turns us into pigs and makes us forget what's important?"

Diodotus, mostly quiet until now, cuts in. "It's not so much the wine itself that causes all the problems, but the fact that we choose to drink too much wine."

Nicias, finished now, shakes his head in agreement.

In the quiet of your own mind you wonder if your friends have grown a bit too serious.

Drowning in Wine

"You're right, though," confirms Diodotus. "Wine ruins a man's judgment. Odysseus claims that too much drinking causes you to sing loudly, laugh like a fool, dance crazily, and say things you shouldn't say. According to his son, too much wine makes your head roll around uncontrollably. And somewhere else one of them claims that excessive wine might lead a group of men to quarrelling.

"That's how they get the suitors to put away their weapons. Remember? If not for that, the suitors might have slain Odysseus and Telemachus. But thanks to the wine and the fact that the suitors are well into their cups, they're all off guard—especially Antinous. It gives Homer the opportunity to indulge in the sort of poetic description he's so fond of. When Odysseus lets fly the arrow from his bow that no one else could string, it goes straight through Antinous' throat. Homer sings, 'He fell over and the cup of wine dropped from his hand, while a thick stream of blood gushed from his nostrils.' His legs kick out, the table topples over, and his life-breath escapes through the barrier of his teeth. Perhaps moderation would have saved him. The strange thing is that he knew better.

"We know this thanks to how Antinous instructs the beggar Odysseus: 'Wine can harm the man who drinks immoderately.' Incidentally, Odysseus is as sober as can be given what he hopes to do shortly (slaughter the suitors). Nevertheless, because Odysseus is behaving like a nobleman instead of the apparent beggar he is, Antinous reasonably suspects he's blitzed with Dionysus' liquid gift. 'Honey-sweet wine harms the man who gulps it down and drinks it beyond measure,' he chides, 'beyond what Fate has given to men.' These are big words from a little man, echoing what Zeus declares in the first book of the *Odyssey*, that the reckless deeds of men lead to their own destruction.

"He goes on to inform Odysseus that the centaur Eurytion was the first to know the dismal pain of drinking too much. That Antinous dishes out this advice is ironic given how much he and the suitors drink. But no matter. He's right. When the glorious centaur was in Pirithous' house, the king of the Thessalian Lapiths, he drowned his heart and mind in wine and did evil to the house of the king.

"During the great brawl that followed, the Lapiths dragged Eurytion outside, cut off his ears and sheared off his nose. 'Thus,' finishes Antinous, 'was begun the great feud between men and the centaurs.' The message to the beggar Odysseus is clear: wine would do the same to him.

"Antinous ends by threatening Odysseus with a one-way trip to king Echetus on the mainland—the sadist king who would skin him alive before killing him. Fat chance, that! In not more time than it takes a man to walk from the Acropolis to the agora, Antinous was bleeding out on the floor. So much for taking his own advice! Drowning in wine, he ended up in a pool of his own blood.

"I'll be briefer with the other two accounts I have in mind from Homer. For poor Elpenor, the mate of Odysseus who fell off a roof and died while drunk, wine was anything but a joy. Aside from bad luck caused by some god, he reports to Odysseus in the Underworld that it was 'a marvelous quantity of wine' that did him in.

"So too was wine the undoing of the human-eating Cyclops Polyphemos. When Odysseus gave him unmixed wine, a particularly rich and strong vintage, Polyphemos was unable to hold back and gulped down Cyclopean quantities. The result? Well right off, like some young man at his first

symposium, he became sick, vomiting all over his cave apartment. Homer tells us that 'presently he turned sick, and threw up both wine and the chunks of human flesh on which he had been gorging, for he was very drunk.'

"That's not all. With the Cyclops knocked out by the wine and fast asleep, his defenses down like our friend Alcibiades over here, Odysseus capitalized on the opportunity to jab a red-hot stake into Polyphemos' sole eye. With that, the Cyclops howled in pain!

"Yes, however good it might be in the right amount and at an apt moment, improper use of wine can spell disaster."[†]

Once again, with the end of Diodotus' speech, Socrates stands up from his couch and heartily cheers for each of the discourses, especially Callias' construction of Odysseus' theory of hunger and thirst—Socrates' word, not that of the son of Hipponicus. He says that he's recently been turning over the very thing in his own mind.

"Odysseus is right, you know. It is the basic urge for food and wine that leads to warfare. No," he corrects himself, "it is more the desire for especially fine food and wine. Gourmet. If only men would settle for simple fare and common wine, then there would be plenty of both. But because we want the best, our own farms and vineyards are no longer sufficient. It's the difference between what

---

† I'm reminded of Paul's admonition to the church at Ephesus that falls in line with earlier Greek and Roman criticisms of drinking too much wine: "Do not get drunk on wine, which leads to debauchery, instead be filled with the Holy Spirit." Drink, yes; but don't get (too) drunk.

Hesiod calls the City of Justice—the city satisfied with what it can produce on its own or acquire through friendly trade—and the City of Crime—the one whose desires propel it to attack others unjustly. Consequently, we create and train armies and navies to attack and plunder the land others possess and use for their own good. We have to, don't we?

"I like to think of these two cities in terms of a city of need and a city of want. In the latter, desire tyrannizes its citizens and despotically subjects others to its own power, whereas the former city is harmonious within itself and peaceful in its relations with other cities."

With his last remark, you see Thrasymachus stirring once again. Socrates asks him what's wrong.

When Thrasymachus strongly asserts again that such forceful behavior is necessary in human affairs and that to call it criminal is itself criminal, Socrates smiles.

"Well, perhaps we can at least all agree that moderation is best for the majority, if not for the few."

"Perhaps," agrees Thrasymachus, cautiously. "Moderation is not only best for the weak majority, but also absolutely necessary. Only the tyrant, the man who is able to satisfy his any and every desire thanks to the power he wields, is in the position do drink immoderately. In fact, this happy man can do whatever he wants to do and however he wants to do it!"

Socrates nods. Not quite a surrender, but a strategic move to outflank the absurd man.

"Fine," he allows. "Let's see, then. Considering immoderation a problem for most, if not for all, and the whole range of other problems that wine brings to the party as unwanted guests, let's finish by exploring how we can overcome the negative effects of drinking wine."

Everyone approves. So that's what you all do.

And without first volunteering, you find yourself speaking next thanks to Hipponicus' generous offer of your services, just like one might volunteer a friend to sponsor a playwright's production during the Dionysia or to fit out and supply a naval trireme during a time of war.

Deliciously Fun Activity No. 9

Track the negative effects of drinking in your own life

You're right. In itself, this activity is *not* deliciously fun. You might as well spend an hour with your therapist, or worse yet (because you actually like your therapist and find her/him helpful), an hour at the dentist (an hour you faithfully fear twice per year).

But seriously. Considering the possible ill effects of wine will help you enjoy Dionysus' precious liquid even more.

And with that, I'll shut up and let you think.

(One more thing, though. Don't forget to make it official and list the negative effects where you'll be able to find and review them later. And be honest with yourself. As Socrates said, parroting the seven wise men, 'Know yourself.')

9

MODERATION
IN ALL THINGS!

Thales of Miletus, Solon of Athens, Pittacus of Mytilene, and others of the seven wise men met together and dedicated the first drops of their great wisdom to Apollo in his dwelling place at Delphi, inscribing in the pronaos the words which everyone now sings, 'Know yourself' (gnōthi sauton) and 'Nothing too much' (mēden agan).

—SOCRATES, PLATO'S *PROTAGORAS*

AFTER CONSIDERING THE matter for a moment and asking the darker Libyan servant to pour you another cup of wine, you start: "Well, it seems to me that given the terms used by Homer, the solution is straightforward. We must simply reverse course.

"Consider it, friends. When you're on a sailing expedition, if going in one direction leads you into the wind or a storm, and, therefore, to a standstill, then you merely have to turn the opposite way if you wish to move again or escape the wind and storm. The same is true with this particular case of immoderation.

"What terms does Homer use? If I remember from my schooldays and every other occasion I've heard him recited by fine rhapsodes like Ion and not so fine like the street performers we hear every day, he uses very distinct words to describe Elpenor, the Cyclops, and Eetion's mistakes.

"As for the first, the young companion of Odysseus claims that *athesphatos oinos* or an 'unutterable amount of wine' did him in. What Elpenor meant to convey was that no one, not even the gods, could express how much wine he drank. So reversal number one: let's make sure we understand and can precisely articulate how much wine we've had.

"Two, we should drink slowly rather than gulping our wine down like the barbarian Cyclops. Homer reports that when Odysseus gave him the wine, Polyphemus quickly drained the cup before asking for more and more. Four times the wild man did this. And each time, when Odysseus brought the wine, the Cyclops tossed it back *aphradia*, 'thoughtlessly.' Rather than drinking thoughtlessly, therefore, we should be mindful of what we are doing.

"Lastly, Antinous accuses the beggar Odysseus of drinking *chandon*, 'greedily, with his mouth wide open.' This leads Odysseus to drink the wine beyond due measure, or as the suitor puts it, not in accord with proper destiny, *aisimos*, that which has been appointed by the gods for a man. Again, we must reverse course. Even when desire compels us to snatch and grab, slow down.

"That's a good start, surely. But let's see … who else among our poets has given good advice about moderation and the most fitting way to drink?"

The Middle of the Road

"Even though we've heard from him so often tonight, I'll begin with Theognis of Megara. Wasn't he the one that advised his young friend Cyrnus to walk along the middle of the road? He said that the middle course is always the best.

"I know, I know he was addressing the deteriorating political situation in Megara. Yet I believe his advice nevertheless applies to drinking. Between the torrential rapids of drunkenness and the dry riverbed of sobriety, the middle way is preferable.

"Elsewhere Theognis laments two demons of drink that oppress wretched mortals: 'thirst and limb-relaxing drunkenness.' He continues by revealing his own strategy of how to deal with them—that he'll turn toward the middle and pass through them both, neither drinking too little nor too much. To finish with Theognis, who seems to have so much to say about the matter—"

"It's because he was a kill-joy! The sod didn't believe any measure of happiness was within a mortal man's reach."

"Didn't Solon categorically assert the same, that 'No mortal is blessed'? It goes along with what I've been arguing all along. Only the gods are *makar*, blessed. This follows from the fact that the gods are all-powerful and can do whatever they want."

"Sure," you allow, before chastising Agathon who spoke first, and more sweetly, Thrasymachus, who seems to believe that most men are miserable unless immensely powerful. (Ah, you reflect, perhaps this explains why

Thrasymachus is generally so miserable. He's got divine power envy. The man needs a therapist!)

You insistently go on:

"But I won't allow you to usurp my position on the *bēma*. If you wish to speak, you must await your turn, following what is fitting."

They both submit, nodding. When you glance at Thrasymachus, you can see that he's blushing. And for a moment, you actually feel bad for him.

"As I was saying, to finish with Theognis, in one of his elegies he most sensibly states that 'to drink too much wine is an evil, but if a man is able to drink with proper knowledge, then it is no evil thing but good.'

"It seems the atomists Democritus and Leucippus explained this well when they argued that we ought to avoid both deficiency and excess, that is, large movements in the body-soul one way or another. For them, steadiness of life was the best, leading to good cheer.

"But how should we achieve such a balance and what is the best amount of wine? Let's begin with Hipponax of Ephesus. We've already heard that, 'People who drink strong wine possess little prudence.' When he said, 'strong wine,' he meant neat wine, that is, wine without the admixture of water. Consequently, if we wish to drink wisely, we'll add water to the *kratēr* filled with sparkling wine. At very least, there should be a one to one ratio, but it's better to add even more water than that.

"Let's back up. Where did this practice of adding water to wine come from? After all, the barbarians who hail from the lands where wine was born don't mix it into their wine.

But isn't that the point? We don't wish to emulate them. Our manliness and discipline defeated the effeminate and undisciplined Persians at Marathon and Salamis. You know what I'm talking about, Hipponicus, don't you. Didn't your own father fight there?"

"He did. As you all know, he was a Marathoner."

"So he knew firsthand what unmixed wine does to a man."

"He did. And they knocked those sorry barbarians back into the water until the Persians drowned in the watery marsh just like they nightly drowned themselves in their strong wine!"

"Thank the gods!" you piously remark. "But getting back to the point and not to lose my line of thought, the poetess Sappho tells us that Achelous, the son of the Ocean and Earth, invented the mixing of wine. Assuming the truth of her assertion, there is no shortage of men who tell us how we ought to mix the water and wine.

"Xenophanes of Colophon, for instance, makes this point: he suggests that we begin with the water in the mixing bowl before adding the wine. But that's not really the traditional way as you all know. So let's forget him. And

let's certainly not go as far as Lamprus did who was water drinker. The gods forbid! Rather, let's begin with the wine.

"Euenus of Paros gives this advice: 'The best measure of Bacchus is neither the most nor the least.' To begin with, then, have your servant pour the right amount of wine into the mixing bowl. How much? you ask.

Let's follow Hesiod, where he gives us a three to one ratio. 'Pour out three parts water—from a clear-running, ever-flowing spring, the current undisturbed—into a fourth measure of wine.'

"To finish the subject of mixing the wine, recall what our cherished friend the physician Eryximachus just said, that Hippocrates advises changing the ratio of water to wine over the course of the year.

"One point is clear from everything we've heard. The skilled man in drinking will drink moderately. As Critias revealed in reference to the Spartans who, though they are our foemen, are nevertheless exemplars of the moderate life: 'There is no day set apart in Sparta to intoxicate the body with immoderate drinking.' Rather, the Spartans only drink enough to produce friendliness, moderate laughter, and cheerfulness.

"In closing, I'll argue this: though drinking *hyper metron*, beyond proper measure, may give one pleasure on the spot, such drinking will end in long-term pain.  I once heard Socrates"—you nod to recognize him, and he nods in return— "make an apt comparison in this regard. He said that short-term pleasure looms large like the columns nearest you in a long colonnade. Sure enough, though, long-term pain is waiting for you at the opposite end, even though it now seems very small, just as the distant columns appear small."[‡]

[‡] Thanks to my oldest son for glancing back at the camera in the above photo of the Parthenon in Nashville, Tennessee. Can you tell?

When you end your speech, and after the praise dies down—with you feeling successful and pleasantly buzzed—everyone turns to Socrates expecting him to lead the chariot of the Sun into the great Ocean River, as they say. Since he proposed the topic for the evening, it is only fitting that he finishes.

Obliging everyone, he does, but only after a moment of quiet reflection.

Moderation and the Soul

"At root, the problem, my dear friends, is the unruly nature of desire, of Eros. Though I believe Hesiod was wrong about many matters in his *Theogony*, he was right when he sang that Eros unstrings the mind, will, and limbs of men. The younger Aphrodite is not far behind him, whispering words of love only to trap the lover in an inescapable net. The only desire that is true and faithful is philosophy, the desire for wisdom.

"To understand our dilemma, we must understand the nature given us by the creating Demiurge. We are each a self-moving, immortal *psychē*, an everlasting soul, that yearns for nothing more than to revolve around What Is, around Being Itself, the Good. Yet instead of engaging in this blessed activity, our souls have fallen into the realm of becoming, into bodies—what some have aptly compared to a prison or a grave.

"Presently, therefore, our natures have become more like a chariot and charioteer speeding after two horses, one good and noble, and the other not. Let me explain what I mean.

"As we know it now, the soul has three parts, each with its own work or function (*ergon*) and virtue or excellence (*aretê*). But what are these?

"A thing's excellence is the means by which it performs its function well; and a thing's function is that which it does well or better than anything else does. For example, although a knife can do many things—it can stab a cut of roasted goat or serve to clean your teeth as Thrasymachus seems to be using his knife right now—a knife's true function, what it does better than anything else, is to cut. From this, it follows that its excellence is sharpness, for only by sharpness does a knife cut well.

"So then, the soul has three parts and all three have a corresponding function and excellence.

"The first and most glorious part of the soul is what I call the rational part. Although some tie it to the chest, I believe it coincides with a man's head—you know, the part that swims with wine if we let it. The function of the rational part is to rule the other two parts. Now our friend

Thrasymachus here may think that it does so as a tyrant to its own advantage. But that's not true. Rather, the rational part's job is to rule the whole soul for the good of the whole man. It does so by means of wisdom, its excellence. I like to say that the rational part is like a shepherd, a good and wise herdsman who cares well for his flock.

"Unfortunately, as I've already revealed, the soul also has a portion that constantly wishes to disobey the rational part. It's called the desiring part. Whereas its proper and healthy function is to desire in the right manner in terms of nutrition and reproduction, it seems frequently to work in an opposite manner. Like the naughty horse I just mentioned, it oftentimes violently takes the charioteer and chariot—the mind and the body—in the wrong direction.

"The desiring part is associated with the groin and the stomach—yes the one that Odysseus called a plague and the bane of men, the one that drives men to attack and plunder one another. This poor part is like a flock of sheep; it is dumb. I say dumb intentionally, men, because the desiring part doesn't stray on purpose. No, no one ever knowingly does wrong. Rather, it strays thanks to ignorance, just as a flock of sheep might stray into a pack of wolves.

"Fortunately, the gods have provided us with another horse, the spirited part of the soul, which is located in the chest. Its job is to enforce the rule of the rational part. It does so not for the sake of power, however, but for the good of the soul. It bravely accomplishes its work by means of fortitude, courage, and heart. Assisting the rational part, the spirited part is like a tenacious, ever-faithful sheepdog.

"So now we've gathered the requisite knowledge to solve the problem. In order for the body and soul, that is, the chariot, charioteer, and horses, to go in the right direction—in this case, in order to drink the right amount so that drunkenness doesn't flood our minds and better judgment leading to all sorts of other problems—it is necessary for the desiring part to listen to and obey the rational part.

"To give an example from Homer, the desiring Odysseus who wishes to listen to the beautiful but deadly Sirens, has to remember the resolution of his former self, the rational part. Prior to reaching the Sirens, this wise Odysseus commanded his men, the spirited part, to tie him to the mast and row on by the Sirens' rocky, treacherous island, with bees wax plugged in their ears. Thanks to this plan, the whole Odysseus endured and survived, making it past the usually fatal Sirens despite the desiring part's burning urge to stop and listen.

"One of the ways to accomplish a similar survival during a drinking party is to establish a drinking captain, a symposiarch, who reigns over how much and in what measure the wine party drinks. If he determines this ahead of the symposium, then those at the party will be well and the party won't devolve to immoderate chaos and petty flyting as so often happens.

"Getting back to the soul, though, if the reasoning part rules the soul as a good monarch, then there will be harmony or justice in the soul, which is the overall excellence of the soul. The parts of the whole will then be moving toward the same goal together like a well-ordered line of ships rather than confusedly sailing in multiple directions all at once as the Persians did at the great naval battle of Salamis.

"When a man achieves this harmonious condition, then he is happy. For as I've often argued, the man who lives well is blessed and happy (*ho ge eu zōn makarios te kai eudaimōn*)."

Done with his speech, Socrates relaxes, bidding the Libyan servant to pour him another cup of wine. Apparently, he's thirsty.

After Hipponicus thanks him, every man—you included—sits quietly for a while as though Socrates' words have been a soothing salve rubbed on to your disturbed souls.

Now it's late at night. Although you had earlier planned to trek across town toward the hill of the Muses to your own two-story townhouse, you now think better of it. You decide to sleep off your drink with the other men and return straightaway to your farm outside the walls in the morning.

Before sleep falls on you or the others, however, Timotheus of Miletus takes up his lyre once again, and the servants pour out many more cups of wine.

After another few hours and the passage of several other conversations and as many cups of wine, and just about the time when Sirius rises from behind the great river at the edge of the earth, everyone begins to fall asleep. The music has long since fallen silent.

Alcibiades, of course, succumbed first, followed by Agathon and Callias. You glance around and see Timotheus sprawled out on a shaggy lamb's wool throw, cradling his lyre. Thrasymachus is next to him, wine cup in hand, finally conquered. Hipponicus is snoring, as are Prodicus and Protagoras. Nicias and Diodotus sleep quietly on couches opposite you. Where is Socrates?

You spot him. As he was at the beginning of the symposium, Socrates is standing in the corner facing the wall, manically rocking back and forth. Thanks to the flickering lamp nearby that throws light toward the corner, you can see his lips barely moving in the shadows. You're certain. He's having one of those famous fits of abstraction, just as he had at the battle of Potidaea, when he stood there lost in thought, struggling with one enigma or another all night long, until sunrise, when he greeted the divine Sun with prayer offerings.

You guess he must be contemplating the ineffable Good he so often talks about but never defines, the indivisible, eternal One of Parmenides, which—.

But with that thought, your eyes grow heavy with wine and exhaustion, and mirroring the others, you fall asleep.

It's the last you remember before waking up.

Deliciously Fun Activity No. 10

Moderation experiment

You may not be convinced of the benefits of moderation. Fine. If not, try a little experiment.

Night one. Drink way too much wine (the amount, of course, will depend on you—your size, level of tolerance, ethnicity, etc.). Note how you feel when you're drinking and how you feel in the morning (how the columns change size). Note also how others experience your drinking and other matters, like how much money you spend.

Night two. Drink a moderate amount of your favorite wine and note the same kinds of things. What do you like about the experience? More than when you drank too much?

Good luck with the experiment. Most importantly, be candid with yourself! *Gnōthi sauton* (know yourself).

All joking aside, you may realize you have to cut back considerably. According to the National Institute on Alcohol Abuse and Alcoholism, 25% of all people 18 and up occasionally engage in binge drinking, and some 7% of the same cohort suffer from an alcohol use disorder (AUD) (aka alcoholism). If this is you, admit it and do something about it. It's not a weakness but a disease; your brain just so happens to be slightly different than other brains.

(On a lighter note, did you notice something wrong with Socrates' feet in the above illustration? Hint: he's like Gerry Fleck, only opposite, the goofy character we all love in the hilarious dog-centric movie, *Best in Show*.)

AMPHORA III

HAPPINESS AND FEASTING
PAST, PRESENT, AND … THE FUTURE

10

ANCIENT GREEK HAPPINESS FORMULAS

Let Telemachus be one of the happy men, may he get what he wants.
—ODYSSEUS, THE *ODYSSEY*

HOLY DIONYSUS! What in the god's name has happened? It's not the headache that bothers you when you wake up. Honest to Zeus. That's nothing a little willow bark and myrtle chased by a cup of cold snow water can't handle.

Rather, it's the overwhelming sense of disorientation you have. You feel out of place, as if you're forever falling like a bronze anvil from the starry sky—down down down past the massive roots of the earth and sea, down to Tartaros, the great Chasm, and the house of Night and Day, and finally down into the darkness of Hades, where the three-headed hound Cerberus wags his tail when you arrive but barks, snarls, and growls when you attempt to leave.[§]

The tumbling sense you feel shifts from an imposing discomfort to a choking fear when you step from the *andrōn* and courtyard and into the street and realize that something is dreadfully wrong. Everything has changed!

[§] Cosmic map courtesy of Hesiod's *Theogony*.

Stifling the kind of scream that usually only manifests in dreams, you return to Hipponicus' house in order to reorient yourself and figure out what the hades is going on. But when you do, you observe that everything is different there as well!

To comfort yourself and bring a measure of calm to mind, you tell yourself that you must have changed houses late at night with the help of your slaves. They must have carried you ... But where? When you find them, you'll have to chastise them. They should know better, messing with you when you're drunk! And dipping into the wine bowl!

Now you find yourself in a large room, about the size of Hipponicus' *andrōn*, but slightly bigger. It's furnished with many low wooden tables and chairs scattered about, and one long and high table at the far end. You don't know what to call the table, but when you look at its surface, the term *aithops* comes to mind. Ten or so benches face it. They're tall and skinny.

Above the high table and around the room are—can it be?—light-casting paintings framed with shiny and very smooth black wood that match the best work you've seen by the rival painters Zeuxis and Apollodorus, only better. Aside from their realism, the astonishing thing is that the images are moving by themselves, with bright yellow Greek words marching across the bottom like a well-ordered phalanx into battle. *Zeus on Olympus!* You can't believe it.

Then there are the lamps. Although they give off light, they don't appear to be fire. Or rather they are a fire, but the flames never seem to move or change place—disproving

Heraclitus of Ephesus, you judge, who said that all is fire, and thus, that all is change.

Behind the high table, there are rows of what look like highly polished oil jars (*lekythos*), wine jars (*oinochoe*), or perhaps even water carriers (*loutrophoros*). You can't say. You've never seen anything like them. On their front, rather than paintings of the gods, men, animals, or plants, there appear to be smooth papyrus tags with small pictures and Greek letters painted in different colors, some of which you've never seen, let alone seen any artist use.

At the end of the high table, you see a man drinking by himself. On the other side is evidently a servant. He's wiping down the table with a soft goatskin rag.

Thankful to the gods to see any mortal at all, you stroll over to the lone man who is wearing a very strange outfit, and you ask if you can sit down on one of the high benches. He tells you that given the fact that you're a human being, you can choose to do anything you like.

"Thanks," you say.

He smiles.

"By the way, what are these called?"

"These?" he laughs, shrugging. "Bar stools, what else?"

Quietly, you wander what a bar is, let alone a stool. You've never heard the words.

Finally, you turn to the man and ask him to answer what you know is a very bizarre question—where you are.

He takes a drink of his wine and answers, "The Philoistron near the Acropolis of Athens. You're in the bar." Then, after a moment, he asks, "Are you okay, friend?"

You don't answer. Rather, when he tells you you're near the Acropolis, you instantly slide off the tall bench and dash out the door in order to catch a glimpse of the propylaea and the Parthenon above, surrounded by all the other temples and structures.

Standing there, time freezes as streams do in the mountains during wintertime.

When you look up and see Athena's temple and the rest of the sacred buildings there, you shudder like one pursued by the fates of death!

O gods! The whole Acropolis is a ruins!

Moments later, you stagger back to the high table and to the tall bench.

Observing your distress, the man orders you a cup of wine. After you drink it and another, you turn to him and ask him what's going on. Are you dreaming?

"No," he chuckles, "I assure you I'm no dream."

"Then where am I?"

"I told you, the Philoistron in Athens near the Acropolis. You're in the bar. Where else might you be?"

It's true, you think. You yourself saw the Acropolis with your own eyes, or at least the ruins. (Gods! Poseidon the earthquaker!) They look like the long walls did when you were very young, when the Spartans pulled them down after the Persian affair. Whatever has happened, time has definitely passed since you last saw the Acropolis.

But *when* are you, you wonder.

Are you still living during the archonship of Diotimus, and the generalships of Demosthenes, Asopius, Paches, Cleidippes, and Lysicles?

And did the Spartans do it? Did they pull down every-thing? Or was it Poseidon?

You ask him.

When you do, he looks at you as if you're out of your mind with Dionysus' blessed gift.

Perhaps you are. *Still.*

Athens, 2014 AD

"It's 2014," he says. "You know," he slowly repeats, as if you don't understand Greek, "two … thousand … fourteen … AD … the … year … of … our … Lord."

"Do you mean the lord Zeus?" you ask, hoping he agrees with at least that.

"Are you kidding me? Look, I'm not much of a believer myself, but—."

"Apollo? Demeter? Athena? Dionysus?" You've desper-ately got to know!

"Jesus, no! I'm talking about the Christ! You know, the one who lived two thousand years ago, five hundred years after the Buddha, Confucius, and Lao Tzu, give or take a few decades."

You do the math. Quickly. And you realize this man is telling you that somehow millennia have passed since you fell asleep in Hipponicus' house.

But how?

Again, you wouldn't believe it except you saw with your own eyes that the Parthenon is now a dull mess of stone, whereas it used to be vibrantly painted and …

But how?!

Perhaps you've journeyed somehow through time? Didn't the poet Orpheus mention the possibility? Isn't that part of the Orphic rites? And if Parmenides is right about the One, about Being Itself, and the fact that there is actually no space or time, and that all change is an illusion, then...

And you look at the flames that don't move in this strange room, this so-called bar, and decide that Parmenides must be right, because how in the god's name does fire not move?!

With this realization, you shiver and conclude you're no longer in *your* Athens.

Uranian gods! What about your wife and children? What about your friends? What has happened? What was in that wine last night?! Did Alcibiades slip in...

Again, the man asks what's wrong after ordering the slave to bring you another cup of wine—a wine, incidentally, that is like nothing else you've ever had from your own vineyard or any other land. It's smooth. There's no salt-water sting. And the aroma! *Sweet Dionysus!*

You consider his question, what's wrong—where and when you are. Finally:

"I don't know," you respond. "I was at a drinking party last night with Hipponicus, Agathon, Alcibiades, Diodotus, Nicias, Callias, Thrasymachus"—you shudder with the usual revulsion, though now you'd even welcome him—"and some others, including Timotheus of Miletus and Socrates the philosopher. But when I woke up this morning—."

He stops you. "With Socrates? The *philosopher*?"

You nod and the man laughs aloud.

"He's been dead for a long time! What were you drinking at that party? Or smoking?"

"*Smoking*? What are you talking about? There was a fire, but ... What do you mean, Socrates is dead?"

"Yeah, Athens put him to death in 399 BC. That's nearly two thousand five hundred years ago. Forced hemlock on the poor man. Haven't you ever read Plato's dialogues—the *Apology* or the *Phaedo*?"

Ignoring this Plato, whom you imagine must somehow be related to Socrates—though on second thought you think he might be the very young child Ariston presented to you at his house recently, claiming he could already do simple math with the help of his fingers and a pile of figs— you jump to the more important point and conclusion:

"Then I *have* travelled through time," you declare. "Parmenides was right."

"What? I didn't say anything about time travel."

You shake your head back and forth. "Whatever you said, when I left Hipponicus' house, Socrates was very much alive, standing in the corner ... thinking."

Again, he laughs. "So, if you know Socrates so well, then tell me what he looked like."

You tell him.

"Okay. But anyone who knows anything at all would know that he looks like a snub-nosed, rather ugly old Silenus. Let's try something harder. Tell me what kind of sandals he preferred."

"You're trying to trick me! He doesn't prefer any. He always goes about barefooted."

"Okay. Is he a lightweight when it comes to drinking?"

"Are you kidding me?"

"Does he enjoy using similes and metaphors?"

"Am I Greek?"

"Fine. One last one. And much harder. Tell me what he believes about the good life. I happen to know a bit about Socrates myself and will tell you if you're right or wrong."

No problem, you think.

But first you have to regain full control of yourself because you still feel somewhat out of your sandals, as they say. You've been in worse situations before, you tell yourself. Naval and land battles. Life and death speeches before the assembly. The ire of your own wife. Changing diapers (okay, you've never done that).

Luckily Socrates just told you and your friends about the good life. You thank Zeus and the other immortals.

After downing a half cup of wine, you pray for a little courage to accept this very strange—what?—vision, dream, hallucination, reality, experience?

Finally, you tell the man about the three parts of the soul, the function and excellence of each, and about the happiness that results when all three parts work together harmoniously.

"He shrugs. Not bad. But I don't think it proves you're not a loon. If you truly come from ancient Greece, and if you actually know the man well, then tell me how he was different from all other men. How did he look at life differently?"

You thank Hermes you can answer this one too. Other men more intelligent and knowledgeable than you have talked about how Socrates' is different for many years now, some in praise and some to blame.

You tell him that whereas other men were interested in the cosmos and how everything came to be, from what basic stuff it came and to what it would return—things such as earth, water, air, and fire, not to mention Pythagoras' numbers and Parmenides' One—Socrates turned the conversation toward human life and what it means to live well."

THE FOUR ELEMENTS

"Are you telling me that he was the first to answer this question?"

Gods, you think. Are you on trial? Why is this man grilling you like you're a leg of goat slowly turning over a fire? All you want to know is where you are and how you can get back to where you were.

And no matter what you've done to calm yourself, you're still disturbed with confusion and fright. It's not quite the same feeling you have before jogging into battle at the head of the phalanx line, but something more like the unnerving sensation you had when your first son was born and the whole world suddenly changed. Except for this feels strange, upsetting, scary, whereas that felt remarkably good.

Even so, drinking another cup kindly supplied by the slave, you oblige the man. Despite his fiery persistence, he seems genuinely curious—the kind of man who probes and asks questions until he finds the answer or admits defeat.

As you speak to him and simultaneously try to calm yourself even as Odysseus or Diomedes did when surrounded by the Trojans in battle, you gradually feel better and forget about your immediate and utterly strange predicament.

Indeed, as you talk about happiness, you actually begin to feel happier.

Ancient Greek Happiness Formulas

Before you begin your exposition of early Greek thinking about happiness, you take a few moments to collect your thoughts in order to marshal your presentation in proper order. Then you start.

"I suppose the earliest formula for happiness can be traced back to Homer's *Odyssey*, just after Telemachus gives Odysseus a gift of roasted meat, hot bread, and a jug of red wine. Just before he eats, he prays that his son may be happy and get what he wants. 'Zeus and you others gods, let Telemachus be one of the happy men; may he get what he wants.'

"The conclusion I draw from Homer, then, is that happiness is the satisfaction of desire. If you have what you desire, then you are happy."

"Like Telemachus' gift of food and wine?"

"Sure."

"Do you mean anything at all?"

"Do *I*?"

"No, Homer."

"Well, no. There is an evident hierarchy of desires in Homer ranging from the merest desire to survive at bottom, including all the things like bread and wine that help a man to survive, to glory at the top, which confers status on a man, and consequently, all the goods he desires to live and do well."

The man nods his head. "Makes sense."

You agree.

But he isn't yet finished. "You've given me the *what* and *why* of happiness," he observes, "but what about the *how*. How do all the heroes in Homer get the good life?"

Without thinking about it, you reply, "Simple. It is by means of competition in power, whether a hero competes individually or in cooperation with his family, friends, and the gods."

Meanwhile, your companion taps the high table, thinking. He eats a few olives and swallows some of his wine before saying, "It seems like you've covered all the essential points. You've given me the *what*—things desired, the *why*—survival and status for survival at one end and thriving at the other, and the *how* of happiness—competition and cooperation. I wonder what more of happiness there can be. I don't believe things have changed all that much, even now."

Why would have things changed, you reflect, unless the world has reverted to the rule of Kronos once again? The way this man talks, however, you judge the world and men must still be trapped in the Iron Age of Zeus, where everyone has to work hard and compete for everything. Considering this, you think of Hesiod, which brings you to the next formula.

"Let's see," you say aloud, "there *was* a slight shift. But very slight. You can discern it in Hesiod's poems. But not his *Theogony*—only in the *Works and Days*. The significant difference is the way you get what you want. Rather than fighting it out in battle or plundering others, Hesiod urges his brother on to hard work that will provide him with all he desires—bread, wine, goat cheese, roasted meat, and so on, all beneath the shade of a tree and with a woman, if, that is, he still has strength for it."

"Why do you mean—*it*?"

"What all women want. Sex. They're animals, you know, like a lioness stealing chickens on a farm!"

The man tilts his head. Slightly. "They are?"

You wonder what's going on with him, how at his age he isn't familiar with women, and so you ask the obvious. "What—do you only like young boys?"

The man laughs, remembering how ancient Athens and Greece used to be. Then he bizarrely claims, "As for women, they're just as likely to accuse men of being like lions as the other way around."

"Oh, you're wrong there. Women can't do without it. In fact, in Sparta and Athens the women have lately conspired to stop having sex until the men stop making war. The problem with their plan? Many have refused, claiming it would be like going without food and wine. Impossible! They have to have it!"

Then the man says something truly strange; he says he wouldn't mind travelling to ancient Greece. Says it would make him happy, satisfy his desire.

"With women?"

"Yeah."

You laugh.

"What else?" he asks, referring to happiness, not women.

"Well, past Hesiod, there were all sorts of formulas for happiness proposed by just as many men. We might call one the sour formula, the one that says no man will ever be happy. Solon believed this.

"Then there's the avoidance formula. I've heard Euripides declare, 'That man is happiest who lives on day after day, escaping misery.'

"And just now, the end of life formula seems very popular. My good friend Herodotus made it famous when he told the story of the wise man who explained to the fabulously wealthy Lydian ruler Croesus that one can only judge happiness (or not) at the end of a person's life. Until then, he said, reserve judgment. After all, who knows what will happen tomorrow?

"I happen to adhere to the half-full formula myself. Someone asks: Can a man be happy? And I answer: Well, yes, but the problem is—.

"Explaining the bad fortune in life that everyone experiences now and again, and how the noble man puts up with it better than the base man, Theognis of Megara gave this over-arching explanation for the half-full formula: 'For no one is wholly happy in every respect ...' Just in some ways. And sometimes.

The man says, "If I were American, I think I might try to bumper sticker that one: *crap happens—sometimes.*"

"American?"

He chuckles. "Never mind."

"Okay," you nod, wondering nevertheless what he's hiding from you and if *American* has anything to do with why you are no longer in your Athens. It sounds like some barbaric Phrygian word.

You go on: "Another is the relativist formula. Just as we say that beauty is in the eye of the beholder, so too does happiness vary from one person to the next. Archilochus of Paros stated, "There is no single kind of human nature, but different things warm different people's hearts.""

"Sensible," the man judges.

"I agree. There are others, too, but they're mostly variations on the first one, that happiness is the satisfaction of desire—for sex, delight, horses, young boys, pleasure, success, wealth, health, glory, and the like. You know?"

"So how did Socrates change things? I mean you said he was the first to think about the good life, but it seems like we Greeks have been thinking about happiness for a very long time."

"True—but he did. Trust me."

"That's exactly what I won't do—no offense. If you make a claim, I'd like you to demonstrate its truth."

Zeus, you think. The man suddenly reminds you of the philosopher himself. On second glance, he looks like him too. It's all too strange.

Thinking of him, you declare, "Socrates shifted things in two ways. One he claimed that happiness was not merely the satisfaction of desire."

"Jesus! How can it not be the satisfaction of desire?"

There's that strange god again, you observe, the one he mentioned earlier. On second thought, you realize the man must only be saying, "*the*-Zeus," with the theta sound overlapping or contracting with the zeta. Who knows.

Anyway, getting back to his counter assertion, you answer, "Look, along with Socrates there are the sophists, wise men who run around Hellas selling their expertise and wisdom. I know many of them and am well acquainted with their beliefs. In short, they hold that happiness is the satisfaction of any and every desire by whatever means necessary. Quite a few consequently believe that the happiest man is the tyrant, since tyrants have the power to get whatever they want. And although this makes sense, Socrates vehemently disagrees with them."

He shrugs. "Why? The idea seems sound to me."

"Me too. But it's not—at least not according to Socrates. The reason has to do with the fact that we are not our own creators. Remember how Socrates said that the creating Demiurge generously gave us a very specific nature that deeply yearns for What is, to know and participate in the life of Being Itself? Well, the sophists deny this nature. Instead, they encourage the desiring part of the soul toward whatever it wants. There's one man who has even admitted that happiness is a mega itch as long as you can scratch it!"

The man laughs aloud. "So if I touch poison ivy, I'll be happy?"

Not knowing what poison ivy is, you shrug, say sure, and go on to Socrates' other point, the one having to do with the nature of what really satisfies.

"Whereas most men up to and including the sophists look to external goods to satisfy desire, and to Fate and the gods as well as their own might to deliver the goods, Socrates claims they have matters inside out. Fate doesn't provide happiness, excellence does. And excellence is a habit a man himself possesses. It's an internal quality or good that is steady and reliable and cannot be taken away at the whims of the gods. It's a state of being not a state of having."

"Speaking of, I feel like I could have another drink."

You join him in another cup.

After a while, he admits that you really must be from another time given how well you know what the ancients thought. Either that or you're a very odd teacher. But he gives up on this idea when you assure him that you've never been a slave and would never condescend to work for free or for any other man, let alone for children. (*The*-Zeus!)

Enjoying the wine, you assure your companion there are many more theories about the good life. Many men, for instance, prize wine as a significant part of what makes us happy for all sorts of reasons, from the pleasure it brings to the health it affords to the courage it lends a man in battle. Which reminds you of Pericles.

"What about him?"

The man claims to know all about the Athenian leader from his time in first through third gymnasium and something he calls university.

Ignoring the latter word *university*, because, once again,

you've never heard it before, you explain, "Pericles said that happiness was freedom from dominance, and that such freedom resulted from courage. Therefore, if wine provided a man with courage, then you could argue that wine is happiness."

The man slaps the high table, chuckles, and leans back on the tall bench.

"Give me another!" he calls out to the slave. "That's a formula I can readily accept. Although Socrates may be right about the soul, desire, harmony, and the Good, wine is a far easier way to be happy!"

You agree. Even though as far as you're aware, you've never revolved around Being Itself, and you don't even know if you have the soul that Socrates professes—though you think you do—one thing you do know: the ecstasy achieved by Dionysus is like no other.

"So what should we do?" asks the man.

"What do you mean?"

"I mean do you want to come join me for more wine and a meal or what? I know a perfect restaurant that specializes in the old food, in the ancient food of Athens. They even serve a dessert they label the Horn of Amalthea or the 'dessert of Zeus' as it was called, and ambrosia, which they claim is nine times as sweet as honey."

You don't believe it. You've always heard of the Horn, but you've never actually seen it, let alone tasted it. And ambrosia? Who but Achilles has eaten the food of the gods? This man has to be drunk. Then again, you think about all the events of the morning—the ruined Parthenon on the Acropolis, the light-casting and moving paintings, and the flames that don't move—and you realize he just may be telling the truth.

"I'll go," you agree.

"Fine. Let's pay up and leave."

The man pulls out a strange rectangle of some unknown shiny gray material with a dark stripe on one side and raised numbers and lettering on the other and gives it to the servant who's been pouring out your wine.

After the servant returns the rectangle with an oblong section of very thin white papyrus and a sea blue stylus that seems to bleed black blood when the man presses on it, and after the man writes his name, you follow him out of the strange *andrōn* and into the streets of this Athens you've never seen before. You know it must nevertheless be your city, though, for the fact that you recognize the temple of Athena Nike and the Theatre of Dionysus in the distance.

That observed, other ruined buildings you've never seen before are there as well, not to mention other kinds of totally foreign architecture and—sweet Hermes!—wagons that move by themselves without horses, and scantily clad women that make your adolescent dreams of Aphrodite and Helen seem like the tame fantasies of an old man.

As you walk out the door into the daylight, the man turns to ask your name. You tell him, even though you can hardly remember it given the circumstances.

After he offers his own, you stroll down a tree-lined pathway past what he claims is the agora—holy Hephaestus, it's also in ruins!—down a street that's called the Adrianou, which, given where it is relative to the agora, must be the Panathenaic Way, past the Kerameikos and toward your own farm. Except for there's no longer any farmland! None at all! Everywhere you look, there are buildings, houses, indoor markets, and the gods know what else. You don't even have words for it all!

Finally, you come to a restaurant that you swear is right where your own farm would have been. You believe this because the right amount of time has passed to reach it—the time it takes you to eat a small loaf of bread and drink a cup of wine.

The restaurant's name is ARCHEON GEFSIS (ANCIENT FLAVORS). A wooden sign out front offers the "authentic fare of Ancient Hellas."

You sigh. However strange it all is, maybe now you'll feel at home inside.

Deliciously Fun Activity No. 11

What's your happiness formula?

Have your friends over for a symposium. Make it a "bring your favorite bottle (or two) of wine" drinking party.

Then, after the small talk is done, the cheese and crackers are half eaten, the hymns are sung, the libations are poured out, and everyone is sufficiently lubed, go around the table or room and share your own formulas for the good life. What is happiness?

If your formula is grand and somewhat ambiguous, try to narrow its parameters as much as possible. If you can, reduce it to its few most important aspects or ingredients.

Afterwards, pour another glass and forget about it.

The hunt for happiness is similar to Orpheus' pursuit of his beloved though perished wife Eurydice in Hades (who died of a snakebite).

After she died, a distraught Orpheus ventured down to the Underworld to demand her back. Seeing his earnestness, and feeling pity like he hadn't felt in millennia, the god of the dead consented to her return, but he did so under this condition: Orpheus couldn't look at Eurydice until they left the realm of the dead.

Guess what happened? Orpheus had her! Eurydice was following him up from the darkness of Hades (read wretched unhappiness) to the light and life of the world of the living (read joyful happiness). They were almost there! But then ... he couldn't help himself.

He turned. And when Orpheus looked back to see if she was coming, Eurydice vanished!

Ovid, the Roman poet who gives us the story, tells us that Orpheus was incredibly depressed after his wife returned to Hades. He didn't want to eat or drink or take a bath. Poor guy.

Anyway, you don't want to hunt too much for happiness. No, as Aristotle said, happiness is something you do, an activity, rather than something you sit around passively thinking about.

11

AN ANCIENT FEAST TODAY

Look, will you point out a few things for me, Heracles, since you've been to Hades before? Like where the rest spots are off the road—you know, like a hotel with prostitutes, a restaurant and bakery, or a drinking hole for wine?
—DIONYSUS, ARISTOPHANES' *FROGS*

B EFORE WALKING IN, the man turns to you and lets you know that he's never been to ANCIENT FLAVORS before. More of a touristy thing, he says. But now that someone from the ancient world is with him—he chuckles, and says he can't get over it—he wants to discover the true nature of ancient fare and if this is it.

Inside, you're surprised to see a set of rooms that seem somewhat ordinary to you, that is, ordinary in comparison to the "bar" you were just in and relative to what you're used to back home in the old Athens. There are Spartan columns flanking a small courtyard (the man assures you they are presently called Doric), ivy decorations with grape clusters, and paintings of the gods and a few people you know, not to mention several of the heroes from Homer.

When he asks you what you think, is it authentic and all that, you tell him that the restaurant is fine for what it is, but the seating arrangement is all wrong. There are far too many tables and far too few couches. And you see no altar to Zeus and the other immortals. Lastly, the torches hanging on the walls still disturb you because the flames are like ice, you say, since they don't move.

"They're electric," he counters.

Before you have a chance to ask what that means, a servant woman offers to seat you at one of the many tables. She's draped in a much nicer tunic than the ones you normally give your slaves. But maybe the Athens of today is wealthier than it used to be.

Just as you settle into a chair, the servant hands you and the man two wide cards of papyrus folded over multiple times to form some kind of geometric pattern that Socrates doubtlessly would be absorbed with if he were here. Your companion calls it a "menu."

Looking at it, you see that Greek words are inscribed on the menu, but not as on a normal scroll, wherethelettersand wordsareallcrowdedtogether like that. Instead, there are spaces between the words making it much easier to read, more organized you can see. (If you ever make it home, you'll have to share this secret with the pedagogues and scribes you know.)

Although reading the menu is a challenge, since the Greek is different from what you're used to, you soon see that the menu-cards are organized into the different courses of the meal. But what are SALATES (SALADS)? The man tells you they are leaf like vegetables and other rabbit food. Which makes you wonder if the new Athens is actually well off. Whatever the case, your mouth begins to water when you see smoked eel, goat cheeses, olives, sausages, and lentils under OREKTIKA (APPETIZERS). On the next page beneath KYPIA PIATA (MAIN DISHES), you're pleased to read all the meats on offer: pig, lamb, oxen, rabbit, goat, deer, chicken, squid, perch, and shrimp, all roasted or stewed. The restaurant must have a whole army of slaves to keep this operation going! Not to mention baking all the GLYCISMATA (PASTRIES AND DESSERTS) and producing all the KRASIA (WINES) on offer. Good Zeus, whether ancient or not, this is going to be a feast to remember for all time!

After some moments have passed, the servant woman comes back and asks you what you would like to drink. You think this is strange. And just before you tell her that it is your custom to eat before drinking, the man orders a jug of red wine. He calls it Avaton and tells you it's from northern Greece near Thessaloniki. You shrug. Once again, as with so many of the words and places he's mentioned, you've never heard of it.

When the servant brings out the Avaton and pours it into two very finely glazed ceramic cups, you do what you customarily do and immediately pour out a libation to the gods onto the floor.

This startles the servant. "What are you doing, sir? Do you not like the wine?"

You tell her you're not sure—you haven't yet tasted it. But when you do, you'll let her know. First, you must sing a hymn to Hestia and to the other gods.

The woman stamps away and returns with something to clean up the wine a moment later, a practice you find out of place since the slaves in the old Athens usually clean up after a party, not during.

While the servant cleans the floor and the man reads the menu, you quietly sing to Hestia while glancing around the  restaurant. On the other side of the room, dressed in a strange tunic you don't recognize, you spot a musician who is plucking a lyre-like instrument. Except the music is not very pleasant. Not only do you not recognize it, but it's far too busy. This makes you wonder if the patrons of the restaurant will sing songs at the end of the feast. When you ask, the man says you can if you want, but he doubts others will. That kind of thing usually only happens on the New Year, he says.

Suddenly, just when you thought you were getting used to things in the new Athens, your tunic nearly falls off—as it were. A whole group of women come in and recline at the table next to yours! What in Gaia's world are *women* doing at a drinking party, you wonder. Furthermore, their soft, patterned tunics hardly cover their breasts, something no respectable woman in your Athens would allow.

Well, seeing the ample cleavage, you're reminded of the breast-shaped cakes Alcman of Sparta reports in one of his songs. He calls them *kribanē mastoeidēs*. (How bizarre.)  All the women in Sparta make them to celebrate the power of the huntress Artemis during their special holidays. At her festival, "they carry them aloft behind the choir when singing in honor of the Maiden."

Although you've never actually seen these breast cakes, you wonder if ANCIENT FLAVORS serves any, and so you ask your new friend.

Unfortunately, when you do, you do so far too loudly. You should have taken into account the women sitting one table over—something you're not used to doing in the old androcentric Athens. Consequently, when you say "breast cakes" in such a way so as to speak over the lyre playing and other noise, they all glance your way, gasp, and proceed to pass their right hands before their bodies as if performing some apotropaic sign to fend off the avenging spirits beneath the earth or some other malady that attacks the chest. They sweep their hands from their foreheads to their bellies, then from their right to left shoulders.

Your friend disabuses you of this superstitious notion when you ask, and tells you that no, they do not serve *breast cakes*, he whispers, at ANCIENT FLAVORS.

Then, with the servant standing unhappily over him, sighing—you think she heard him despite his best effort to be quiet—he orders.

If she were your servant, you would let her know not to eavesdrop. But everything is forgotten, if not forgiven, with the food.

You begin with a plate of greens, goat cheese, and bread served with olive oil and vinegar. Exquisite. Doubtlessly the gods on Olympus do not fare better, even if their weather is superior.

Next, the servant brings black olives, cut sausages, and another jug of wine, this time, NOTIOS RED or THE SOUTHERNER. When you ask your friend why it is called that, the man tells you it's because the wine is from the Peloponnese.

Then it hits you again as it earlier did at the bar. Every wine you've had so far tastes different from anything you've ever had. For a moment, you wonder if you're drinking nectar. There's no taste of resin and the wine is far less salty.

When you tell him, the man asks if you prefer a resinated wine, a retsina, and you assure him you're more than pleased with his choices so far.

Then you notice the papyrus label on the wine jug. On it are inscribed the words, Ktema Gaias (Gaia Estate). It makes sense, but it's news to you. As far as you're aware, Hesiod never sings of it nor does any other poet you've ever heard.

When you ask your friend where Mother Earth's estates are located, he laughs. She doesn't have any estates; it's just the name of the vineyard that makes the wine.

"But Gaia owns the vineyard?"

"No. Ordinary mortals do."

"What about …"

Just as you prepare to ask another question, the snippety servant woman and two others bring out a wooden tray carrying silver plates full of roasted goat garnished with leeks and mashed chickpeas, fried rabbit topped with onions and herbs, and a small ceramic pot of lentil stew. Delicious!

When in order to see how authentic Ancient Flavors is, you ask the servant how the goat was slaughtered, and whether it was first anointed with wine, and which of the gods were honored as the bronze blade severed its life's cord, she looks at you like you're already well and drunk—

especially when your friend orders another jug of wine, a second from none other than Mother Earth's estates.

Slipping into waitress mode and recalling the script written by the owners of ANCIENT FLAVORS, particularly the part dealing with drunk patrons, the servant does her best Dionysian acting job and replies, "You may be certain, sir, that the chefs sacrificed and roasted the goat just as Pericles himself would have done during the Golden Age."

Abruptly, scooting your chair back, you protest. "But Pericles never cooked a thing in his life! That's what slaves are for. And in case you didn't know"—you spot a chance to take a dig at this slave—"he didn't live in the Golden Age. No, his was the Iron Age, just like yours and mine. But unlike *your* lowly life, his glorious life ended when he sacrificed it to the plague for Athens."

The servant doesn't know what to say. You've clearly won. Rather, she raises her eyebrows, smiles, and walks away with the other servants, leaving the two of you to enjoy the delightful fare and wine (that, incidentally, another servant brings out after some time).

Then comes time for the dessert. You remind your friend that he promised ambrosia back at the bar, the food of the gods. Your mouth waters as you imagine something nine times the sweetness of honey. *Gods!*

Then your spirit falls. He tells you that he was just playing with you.

"Joking with me?"

"Yeah."

"Well, what about the Horn of Amalthea?"

"Not even that."

Instead, he orders something all too familiar.

When a manservant brings out figs, Persian walnuts, and Attic honey, you're disappointed, though it does remind you of what your own wife and servants would serve at home. For what it is, though, it's good.

Afterwards, everything seems to sour.

When you finish dessert accompanied by an OIKONOMOU SITIA from Crete, a sweet wine you like very much—but then again, at this point, you'd just as well like any wine, even the kind the common people drink—you once again do what you might ordinarily do toward the end of a symposium.

First, you make a target with an upside-down water cup (yes, they drink water neat in the new Athens) and the saltshaker on the other side of the table. Then, when you drain your cup to the bottom, you begin flicking drops of wine at the target opposite you.

"What are you doing?" the man asks, bemused.

"I'm playing kottabos, what else?"

Flicking with greater purpose now, you make a series of wishes. You desire to return home to *your* Athens, and to Hipponicus' *andrōn*, and to all your friends, and to Socrates standing against the wall contemplating. After that, you want to visit your own farm and stroll through your own vineyards. Then once you watch the slaves tread the grapes in the vats and draw out the wine into the storage jars, you wish to enter your house and make love to your wife. At the thought of it, you flick the wine with eager intent, earnestly wishing the drops toward the target that will secure for you your amorous intent.

As you do so, sweat beads atop your head, and your new friend cracks up watching you. He's never seen anything so hilarious.

If only the servant felt this way, the one who hasn't spoken with you since the mention of Pericles and the sacrifice. Now she's clearly exasperated. And stomping over, she demands to know why you are flinging wine—good wine, sir—all over the table. *You can't do that!*

When you protest and inform her that in ancient Athens—your birth home and the city to which you claim citizenship going back hundreds of years *on both sides*—playing kottabos is customary and what you always do at the end of a feast, she orders you and your friend to leave.

"Leave?"

"Yes, sir."

You're angry now. How can this slave order you around? Although you're generally mild-mannered and actually a lenient fellow, you have in mind a good beating for her. (A one that even Cleon might be proud of.)

Fortunately, your new friend stops you. Knowing you're drunk and just having fun, and attempting to calm everything, the man suggests that you were just getting ready to leave anyway. The food was excellent, he says, complimenting her and the restaurant.

She hardly smiles at this or when he gives her the gray rectangle with the dark stripe.

"What's up with her?" you ask. "Shouldn't we—"

"I'll tell you when we get outside."

Moments later, after the man pays, you leave ANCIENT FLAVORS and step out onto the street.

But my gods!

Sweet *the*-Zeus! (Yes, for the second time since you've been with him, you use the man's strange oath.)

When you enter the street, you immediately realize that you're no longer in the new Athens, but yours, the *old* one.

Quickly, when you pivot around to read the name of the restaurant again and the sign that promises ancient food, you see that you're standing in the entryway to Hipponicus' courtyard.

To your side is Socrates. How? you wonder. He's giggling to himself like a schoolboy.

"What?" you ask, though you really don't want to.

"Nothing," he responds. "I'm just happy. It is morning, the sun is shining, and I can't imagine anything better."

Better? you think. Perhaps a cup of wine.

Well anyway, you're pleased to be home. Whatever happened, it must have been the wine from the night before. And indigestion. And sleeping in a house not your own.

Turning away from Socrates after bidding him farewell, you walk toward your farmhouse just outside the walls rather than to your townhouse.

When you arrive, your wife and servants are preparing a feast for you, your sons, and your one daughter to thank the gods that your farm was spared one more summer from the Spartan enemies that Athens has been fighting for some four years plus now.

You say hello to them all and ask your son how the vineyard's doing. He looks at you like something's wrong, knowing you walked through it just yesterday. You decide to tell him everything later.

For now, pulling your wife by the arm, you tell her the servants can get by on their own for a while. You explain you've made a wish while playing kottabos, one you believe the gods will soon fulfill.

I'm not going to lie. They do.

Deliciously Fun Activity No. 12

Have an ancient Greek feast

Have your friends over for an ancient Greek Feast. No more than about eight to ten people.

First, research authentic Greek dress and make sure everyone shows up in something that at least passes for ancient wear. (On this note, don't get the Greeks mixed up with the Romans. This is not a toga party! In general, ancient Greeks wore the *chitōn*, a long rectangular tunic, which frequently appears in both the *Iliad* and *Odyssey*.)

Second, place couches around a room that's big enough (if you have one) to hold the couches (one person per couch unless you want to double up). Don't be afraid to squeeze. The couches should be set up in a U pattern.

If you do not have so many "couches," make them. Place two to three couch cushions on the floor and cover these with a blanket or some kind of thick covering. Borrow extra cushions if necessary.

Third, assign some of your friends to be servants. Okay, if this doesn't work, then serve the food yourself with their help. Perhaps in shifts. Or just alone.

You should also ask which of your friends plays guitar well enough to have some live music (assuming they can pick up some Greek tunes). If no one plays guitar, buy a few Greek music CDs. I recommend *Putumayo Presents Greece: A Musical Odyssey* (modern Greek music) or Petros Tabouris' *Music of Greek Antiquity*. The latter has hymns to Apollo, the Muses, the Sun, and to Nemesis just in case any of your guests behave foolishly with hubris.

Next, serve the food and wine.

Although there are many good cookbooks out there, I suggest you take a look at the following. For ancient Greek food ideas, see *The Philosopher's Kitchen: Recipes from Ancient Greece and Rome for the Modern Cook* (by food historian Francine Segan), and *Meals and Recipes from Ancient Greece* (by the archaeologist Eugenia Ricotti). For more modern Greek cuisine, check out *The Complete Book of Greek Cooking: The Recipe Club of St. Paul's Orthodox Cathedral* (by the good people at St. Paul's).

For a detailed list of modern Greek wines (including some wines based on ancient methods and styles), see *Divine Vintage*, pgs. 214-239 (you may find its bibliographical information in WORKS THAT INSPIRED DRINKING WINE toward the back). The authors of *Divine Vintage* give wineries, website addresses, grape varieties, official quality of the wine (including an explanation of the Greek appellation system), alcohol content, and their expert impressions. *C'est magnifique!*

Remember, the Greeks ate before drinking, but if you wish to drink while you eat, I'm sure the gods will forgive you. Just make sure you mix a little water into your wine.

Speaking of, don't forget to pour out libations to the immortals before you drink. It goes without saying that your hands should be clean! Then sing a few hymns. Aside from those on the rockin' Tabouris' CD you now possess, you may discover readily accessible hymns among the various collections of *Homeric Hymns* online. There you'll encounter hymns to Hestia, Zeus, Apollo, Demeter, Hera, Pan, the Earth Mother, Dionysus, and all your other favorite gods. If this doesn't excite you, then write your own (it's what the Greeks did). If you do, be sure to beg inspiration from the Muses first. Start off with, "Sing Muses, of [*the god here*], who..." And so on.

By the way, I didn't mention anything about anointing the goat or lamb with wine before you sacrifice it. This is a bit tricky, assuming you're not actually slaughtering the animal (as many Muslims still do on Eid al-Adha, for example, the holiday celebrating Abraham's willingness to sacrifice Isaac—the same willingness Søren Kierkegaard enshrines in his famous "leap of faith"). What I suggest, then, is that once you've removed the cut of meat from the white styrofoam holder and plastic wrap, you place it in a colander and anoint it in the sink. You can even cut it some and make *baaing* and *mehing* noises if you please.

Don't forget to set aside some fat for the gods. (Remember, they called it.) And if the oven starts smoking while you're roasting the animal, open it up and let the gods have their fill. They love that smoky stuff!

After eating and drinking, it's time to sing and play games. Having done all the deliciously fun activities, I know you've already played a round or two of kottabos. So unless you're really hankering for another game, try something else. Try singing some party songs. If you really want to go Greek (you should), you can consult a variety of English translations of ancient Greek Lyric poetry—the songs they would have sung at their own parties (Martin L. West's one volume translation from Oxford or David A. Campbell's five volumes from the Loeb collection will do, as well as the Loeb Iambic and Elegiac collections; there are also online editions).

By this point, you've consumed much wine and are well on your way to being tanked—though you have no plan to go into battle.

The question: do (you all) stay or do you go?

Whatever you do, learn more about wine.

And may the gods, including the happiest, most charming divinity Dionysus, bless you in your every endeavor.

So be it.

ACKNOWLEDGEMENTS AND GRATITUDE

*When they had poured out drink offerings to the everlasting gods with
gratitude, each drank as he desired...*

—HOMER, THE *ODYSSEY*

Thanks so much for reading *Drinking Wine with Homer & the
Earliest Greeks*!

While you're at it, will you go to Amazon (or wherever
you bought the book) and leave a positive review? *Sas
eucharistō* (thank you)!

I hope you learned much while reading, drank a lot
(moderately, of course, and with greater appreciation),
enjoyed yourself, and put up with my odd sense of humor (a
one my wife has to tolerate on a regular basis).

Speaking of, my gratitude always belongs first with my
own dear Hera, though she is much more of a Semele to me
and most definitely *not* my sister. I thank her and also my
children for enduring my absence while I manically hammered out and illustrated *Drinking Wine* for hours upon
countless hours at a time.

Although I must recognize Homer and all the early
Greek poets for their insightful reflections on drinking
Dionysus' liquid gift, there are several modern authors who
deserve my special gratitude. Foremost is the so-called
Indiana Jones of wine archeology, Patrick E. McGovern. If

I were Zeus, I would rapture him straight to Mount Olympus and make a god of him, even as Heracles was divinized after his twelve labors.

Next up, I have to thank Moses Finley (author of *The World of Odysseus*) and Martin Litchfield West (author and translator of *everything* classics related) who are two of the most significant gods in the pantheon of Classical Studies (though I leave out many others!). When (and if) I ever reach the Isles of the Blessed, I want to chill with them even before I throw spears with Achilles or catch a glimpse of Nausicaa (my Homeric epic crush). Meanwhile, I'd like to meet M.L. West before he goes to be with the gods. And while we're at it, P.E. McGovern.

Thanks again!

And see you at the bottom of the wine jar!

Tim J. Young
December 2014—Sugar Land, Texas

WORKS THAT INSPIRED
DRINKING WINE WITH HOMER
AND THE EARLIEST GREEKS

Aside from Homer (the book's primary source), Hesiod, and other early Greek authors (mentioned throughout the text), the following more recent works inspired *Drinking with Homer and the Earliest Greeks.**

Burkert, Walter. *Greek Religion.* Translated by John Raffan. Cambridge: Harvard University Press, 1985.

Finley, M.I. *The World of Odysseus.* New York: New York Review of Books with Viking Penguin, 1982.

Fowler, Robert et al. *The Cambridge Guide to Homer.* Cambridge: Cambridge University Press, 2004.

Grace, Virginia R. *Amphoras and the Ancient Wine Trade.* Athens: American School of Classical Studies, 1979.

Graziano Breuning, Loretta. *I, mammal: why your brain links status and happiness.* Pomona: System Integrity Press, 2011.

Grimal, Pierre. *The Penguin Dictionary of Classical Mythology.* London: Penguin Books, 1991.

Hale, John R. *Lords of the Sea: The Epic Story of the Athenian Navy and the Birth of Democracy.* New York: Viking, 2009.

Heskett, Randall and Joel Butler. *Divine Vintage: Following the Wine Trail from Genesis to the Modern Age*. New York: Palgrave MacMillan, 2012.

Kramer, Matt. *Making Sense of Wine*. Philadelphia: Running Press, 2003.

McGovern, Patrick E. *Ancient Wine: The Search for the Origins of Viniculture*. Princeton: Princeton University Press, 2003.

———. *Uncorking the Past: The Quest for Wine, Beer, and Other Alcoholic Beverages*. Berkeley: The University of California Press, 2009.

Matyszak, Philip. *Athens on 5 Drachmas a Day*. London: Thames and Hudson, 2008.

Nilsson, Martin P. *Greek Folk Religion*. Philadelphia: University of Pennsylvania Press, 1972.

Palmer, Leonard R. *Mycenaeans and Minoans: Aegean Prehistory in the Light of the Linear B Tablets*. New York: Alfred A. Knopf, 1962.

Pellechia, Thomas. *Wine: The 8,000-Year-Old Story of the Wine Trade*. New York: Thunder's Mouth Press, 2006.

Standage, Tom. *A History of the World in 6 Glasses*. New York: Bloomsbury, 2005.

*Unless noted, all translations are my own. The Aesop epigram, "The Vine and the Goat," is George Fyler Townsend's rather Victorian translation.

ABOUT THE AUTHOR

After studying undergraduate history and theology for a master's degree in graduate school, Tim J. Young taught for many years and just as many subjects before turning to writing full-time.

He now lives in Sugar Land, Texas with his wife and four children. Although they've considered adding a dog and a cat to the mix, they've never managed more than a hamster, a few zebra finches, a wild lizard, a Venus flytrap, and several versions of a red beta fish (all named Tomato).

Please visit Tim's website, www.timjyoung.com, in order to see what else he's working on or just to drop him a note.

Also by Tim J. Young

The One, the Many
A Novel of Constantine the Great, Athanasius of Alexandria, and
the Battle to Unify the Roman Empire
and the Christian Church

A Hero's Wish
What Homer Believed about
Happiness and the Good Life
(Available mid-January 2015)

Otherwise, Tim is working on and should have the following books out in 2015:

The Four Ships of Homer
How the *Iliad* and *Odyssey*
Will Help You Sail a Happier Life

and

The Break Room
A Comedy
(a novel exploring the much-trumpeted distinction
between religion and spirituality)

10558110R00119

Printed in Great Britain
by Amazon.co.uk, Ltd.,
Marston Gate.